The Behavioral Economics of John Maynard Keynes

T0327344

The Behavioral Economics of John Maynard Keynes

Microfoundations for the World We Live In

Ronald Schettkat

Professor of Economics (em.), Schumpeter School of Economics, University of Wuppertal, Germany

Edward Elgar
PUBLISHING

Cheltenham, UK • Northampton, MA, USA

Cover image of John Maynard Keynes: International Monetary Fund, Public domain, via Wikimedia Commons.

Published by
Edward Elgar Publishing Limited
The Lypiatts
15 Lansdown Road
Cheltenham
Glos GL50 2JA
UK

Edward Elgar Publishing, Inc.
William Pratt House
9 Dewey Court
Northampton
Massachusetts 01060
USA

Paperback edition 2023

A catalogue record for this book
is available from the British Library

Library of Congress Control Number: 2022946670

This book is available electronically in the **Elgar**online
Economics subject collection
http://dx.doi.org/10.4337/9781802204896

ISBN 978 1 80220 488 9 (cased)
ISBN 978 1 0353 2921 2 (paperback)
ISBN 978 1 80220 489 6 (eBook)

Printed and bound by CPI Group (UK) Ltd, Croydon, CR0 4YY

MIX
Paper | Supporting
responsible forestry
FSC® C013604

Contents

Figures

Tables

1. Introduction to *The Behavioral Economics of John Maynard Keynes*

1.1 KEYNES AND BEHAVIORAL ECONOMICS?

Keynes' theory is typically equated with macroeconomics with the relations between aggregates, but Behavioral Economics focuses on individual behavior, which is microeconomics.[1] Do Keynes' theory and Behavioral Economics have anything in common, or are they unrelated? Keynes' theory is often limited to macroeconomics, neglecting its microeconomic foundations, and for long, microeconomics remained neoclassical,[2] often described as schizophrenia in economics because the two do not fit.

All economic theories are behavioral since they analyze economic decisions and actions of humans embedded in societies' norms and rules. However, economic theories differ sharply by the degree of abstraction from observable behavior. Some apply an axiomatic approach and deduce economic behavior from a few assumptions, such as individual maximization of utility or profits, often described as rational. Together with other fundamental concepts—equilibrium, competition, completeness of markets—they derive powerful implications for the constructed

---

[1] Behavioral Economics is here not restricted to researchers who explicitly classify themselves as behavioral economists but it comprises also authors who emphasize the necessity of descriptive content of economic theory.

[2] Keynes used classical or orthodox to distinguish his theory. Although classical is not identical with neoclassical, the latter commonly fits what Keynes refers to as classical as he includes "(for example) J.S. Mill, Marshall, Edgeworth and Prof. Pigou" (Keynes 1936: 3, footnote 1). Often general equilibrium model, Walrasian system, perfect market model, traditional model, standard model, mainstream model, rational rate theory, or simply economic theory are used as synonyms to describe the neoclassical model.

"perfect" system, such as the claim that it achieves the welfare optimum. However, the derived implications rest on many assumptions. They are criticized for the high degree of abstraction, which allows for the logical deductions but which are at odds with the intentions and abilities of humans and markets (Arrow 1986).

Behavioral Economics follows a different approach strongly influenced by psychological and neurological research methods. It attempts to be descriptive to actual observable rather than hypothesized economic behavior. It includes approaches and findings of neighboring disciplines (psychology, neural sciences, sociology, political science) and allows for the analysis of axioms that are not investigated but simply assumed in the axiomatic theories. In Behavioral Economics and Keynes' theory, economics is required to relate to the motivations and abilities of humans to be classified as applicable for economic policy.

Keynes' microeconomic reasoning is based on observed actions of humans as entrepreneurs, workers, consumers, and investors, and this is the fundamental methodological commonality of Keynes and Behavioral Economics, which at the same time distinguishes them from the neoclassical approach. Although Keynes' microfoundations were ignored mainly, they are the basis for his macroeconomic conclusion.

> About two thirds of the *General Theory* deals with the theory of the action of agents, their motives for saving and for holding money, their investment and speculative behavior etc. It is a consequence of intellectual coarseness and not of Keynes that University syllabuses are so frequently divided into watertight macro- and micro-courses. [...] Keynes argues that the actions of agents in markets would not result in the equilibrium posited by his predecessors. It is hard to see how this very important proposition is to be understood without micro-theory. (Hahn 1977: 34)

Howitt (1986) confirms and argues that Keynes' *General Theory of Employment, Interest and Money* (1936) is devoted to microfoundations of macroeconomics, a challenge to the neoclassical concept of how markets function.

Keynes used "general" in the title of his major book to challenge the neoclassical model's optimal and unique equilibrium and make it a very special case of his theory. The *General Theory* is indeed general in two aspects: (1) it covers the full employment equilibrium of neoclassical economics as a special case, and (2) it is based on microeconomic behavior, of which the socially isolated, self-interest maximizing *homo oeconomicus* of neoclassical economics is, at best, a very special case.

Consequently, this book argues that Keynes' micro has a lot in common with Behavioral Economics, a long-neglected but currently flourishing area in economics. Here Behavioral Economics will not only comprise research which explicitly classifies itself as such but also contributions in institutional economics, analysis, tests of economic behavior, and so on. Every economic theory is behavioral, but theories are distinguished by how close their theoretical assumptions of behavior coincide with the observable behavior of humans. Even neoclassical models based on *homo oeconomicus*—the omnipotent artificial figure, a robot (Frydman & Goldberg 2011)—are behavioral, but in a very specific and very narrow manner, far away from the abilities and actions of humans. The behavioral assumptions, however, are so abstract that a new branch of economics emphasizing actual observable behavior in the real world was labeled Behavioral Economics. The new element in Behavioral Economics is its openness to humans' actual decision-making and actions, which it shares with Keynes' approach in the *General Theory*. The major difference between Behavioral Economics and Keynes' *General Theory* on the one side and the neoclassical approach thus lies in the abstraction from actual behavior applied in the theories. The fundamental methodological difference is the distinction between the axiomatic approach of neoclassical economics, which allows ignoring other neighboring disciplines (such as psychology, sociology, political science, but also—more recently—neurology).

Although *microfoundations* became identified with maximization and rational choice, with neoclassical micro, the very meaning is to understand better how humans act as entrepreneurs, consumers, investors, and speculators and what motivates their actions. Neoclassical economics simply assumes utility maximization but is quiet about what is precisely to be maximized and how that maximization is achieved; hence, it takes an axiomatic approach. In contrast, Behavioral Economics does not deduce behavior from artificial behavioral axioms and takes a descriptive approach. Keynes' microfoundations are based on his observations of decisions and circumstances of humans in an economy where money is not simply a veil covering a barter economy as in the classical dichotomy, but where money may be used for savings, speculation, or as a precautionary device affected by expectations in an uncertain world.

The micro–macro split in economics led Lucas and Sargent (1978) to declare that the predictions of the Keynesian theory "[...] were wildly incorrect and that the doctrine on which they were based is fundamentally flawed [...]" (Lucas & Sargent 1978: 49). They claimed that there is only one economics, which needs to be based on neoclassical microfoundations, that is, in their view, maximization and equilibrium.[3] This book argues that the allegation of the missing microfoundations in Keynes' theory is false, as is the assertion that Keynes only removed the *deux ex machina*—the Walrasian auctioneer—from an otherwise neoclassical model (Leijonhufvud 1967). On the contrary, Keynes' microfoundations derived from observations lead to his macroeconomics. They refer to *the world we live in*, to the actual behavior of humans, just as Behavioral Economics does.

1.2   ECONOMIC REVOLUTIONS

How do we navigate the overly complex economy? How do we decide on consumption, work, investments? How do we interact in markets? How do markets function? To better understand these overly complex issues, simplifications, narratives, and theories focusing on the relevant relationships are needed. It is also important to note that "...the ideas of economists and political philosophers, both when they are right and when they are wrong are more powerful than is commonly understood. Indeed, the world is ruled by little else" (Keynes 1936: 383). Economic ideas, theories, and narratives shape our understanding of economic relationships, policy options, and achievements. How do economists develop their theories? One way is to develop their ideas and theories by observing and investigating the motivations and behaviors of economic units (i.e., individuals, firms) and their interactions in markets and society. On that basis, generalizations of economic behavior are then developed with descriptive content, which is Keynes' and the Behavioral Economics' approach, aiming to understand *the world we live in* and develop a theory applicable to it. This is also the approach of real sciences like physics and biology. Another way of theorizing is to begin with assumptions regarded as obvious and true without investigating them (axioms) and deducing economic behavior from these axioms. This is the neoclassical approach as applied in mathematical and logical sciences.

Unfettered markets will steer the economy to maximum welfare—the optimum, but governments and regulations, on the other hand, disturb

---

[3]   Commenting on Lucas and Sargent (1978), Robert Solow (1978) argued that assuming the economy to always be in a state of equilibrium is false. Maximization is meaningless, unless it is specified what is to be optimized.

the smooth market process. This hypothesis continues to dominate neoclassical economic thinking, although it was substantially shaken by the appearance of Keynes' *General Theory*, questioning the automatic, self-regulating mechanism to achieve the welfare optimum proclaimed in the *General Equilibrium*[4] model. The real economy functions at the micro and macro levels differently than deduced from axioms in the neoclassical model. Individuals behave differently, and markets function differently. The neoclassical axioms simply do not apply to *the economy we live in*. Keynes' *General Theory* revolutionized economic thinking and shook the fundaments of the neoclassical model, which became an exceptional case in the new theory. Revolutionary ideas are challenging for people who shape their thinking and arguments in terms of the old framework and are hard to digest.

Therefore, many commentators questioned Keynes' *General Theory* or interpreted it in familiar neoclassical assumptions. This way, they turned the *General Theory* into a particular case of the neoclassical model, ignoring Keynes' insights into individual economic behavior and market functioning. The *General Theory* releases economics from the artificial omnipotent *homo oeconomicus*, allowing for more than one equilibrium. The economy may not turn automatically to the optimum, to full employment but may rather get stuck at suboptimal equilibria. Keynesian macroeconomics is based on microfoundations deviating from perfect rational decision procedures and a broader motivation of humans than deduced from the neoclassical axioms and takes a realistic approach to the functioning of markets.[5] "Indeed, the General Theory was devoted to what would now be called micro-foundations of macro theory" (Howitt 1986: 628). And Hahn (1977) argues that Keynes' macroeconomic conclusion (the possibility of nonoptimal equilibria) rests on the behavior of economic agents diverging from the *homo oeconomicus*. But neoclassical microeconomics was left untouched and untroubled, and Keynes' theory was separated off into a special *macro* branch (Galbraith 1987) with severe consequences for economic policy. Obvious devia-

---

[4] *General,* in the *General Equilibrium* model, refers to equilibrium in all markets.

[5] The interpretation of the *General Theory* was strongly influenced by Hicks (1937), where he neglected uncertainty and constructed a mechanical relationship between the money-supply, interest rates and investments and where he equated Keynes with the "liquidity trap" and labeled it as an extra case (Kromphardt 2013).

tions from neoclassical axioms are often described as imperfections or anomalies, although anomalies are the rule (Krueger 2018) rather than the exception.

Also, many Keynesian economists focused on macro, largely ignoring micro leaving neoclassical microfoundations untouched, which paved the way for the neoclassical counterrevolution that is most visible in *natural rate theory* (Phelps 1968, Friedman 1968) and *rational choice theory*. *One-equilibrium economics* was back in macroeconomics, especially when UK Prime Minister Thatcher (i.e., 1979 through 1990) and US President Reagan (i.e., 1981 through 1989) came into power. Consequently, the neoliberal model championed economic policy after the 1980s, infecting not only neoliberal but also social-democratic politicians, which illustrates well the importance of economic theory for our thinking. Policy, the government, was now identified as the problem, not as part of the solution. The resurrection of *homo oeconomicus* in natural rate theory choosing the optimal leisure-employment and hence "unemployment" is a fabulous illustration of the axiomatic logical versus the real science approach in economics. It also illustrates how easily researchers deeply rooted in the axiomatic approach accept weak empirical evidence in favor of their axiomatic theory as strong support, of which Friedman's Nobel Prize Lecture is a prime example. The *natural rate of unemployment* became the yardstick, the new full employment level, for economic policy. It diffused deeply into the thinking of economists, international organizations, and political parties of almost any orientation.

Mostly unnoticed by the wider public developed an experimental approach to the analysis of individual economic behavior called Behavioral Economics, which aims to describe human decision-making more realistically. *The world we live in* is populated by *humans* and not by fictitious *Econs* (Leijonhufvud 1973). Therefore, Behavioral Economics produced substantial evidence that individual economic behavior deduced from the neoclassical axioms differs fundamentally from individuals' actual motivation, ability, and action in *the economy we live in*. The experimental findings are astonishingly congruent with Keynes' casual microeconomic observations, and they may be the seeds of the next shift in economic thinking for the next economic revolution. Although many behavioral economists are keen to frame their work as an expansion or enrichment of the neoclassical model rather than as an alternative, the findings are revolutionary in that they contradict the neoclassical model's core axioms.

1.3 KEYNES' ECONOMIC REVOLUTION: HUMANS, MARKETS, MONEY

Keynes was very well aware that *The General Theory of Employment, Interest, and Money* (1936) would revolutionize how the world thinks about economic problems. He emphasized his revolutionary ambition with the provocative title, *General Theory*, degrading the neoclassical or General Equilibrium model to his theory's special case. "We are thus led to a more general theory, which includes the classical theory with which we are familiar, as a special case" (Keynes 1936: XXIII). Although Keynes wrote his book to contribute to economic theory, he was very well aware that it would have profound consequences for economic policy, because theory frames our thinking and shapes our view on economic possibilities.

Keynes argued that the optimistic conclusion of the General Equilibrium model that the economy achieves the welfare optimum (i.e., full use of all resources, full employment) only holds under very specific conditions, not applicable to *the world we live in*. In actuality, the economy can balance below the optimum without an automatic mechanism to release the economy from a suboptimal level. He challenged the fundamental assumptions of the neoclassical model, its axioms, but not the deductions based on these assumptions. The critique ranges from the motivation and decisions of socially embedded individuals as workers, entrepreneurs, consumers, and speculators to market processes in a monetary economy. The nonacceptance of the neoclassical axioms leads to rejecting its deductions of economic behavior and their consequences for economic analysis (full employment equilibrium). Keynes' macroeconomic insights are based on his observations of individual economic behavior, that is, on his theory's microfoundations. The intention, ability, and environment contrast with the neoclassical assumptions of social isolation, maximization equated to rationality, the full employment equilibrium, methodological individualism, timeless analysis, ergodicity, and the neutrality of money.

Keynes' theory does not exclude full employment, the optimal equilibrium, but he argues that it is exceptional; there is no automatic mechanism to the optimum. Consequently, Keynes concluded that the *invisible hand* would not automatically steer the economy to the welfare optimum (full employment), as assumed in the neoclassical model. Instead, the economy may get stuck in suboptimal equilibria (underemployment)[6] without an automatic mechanism leading to the optimum. Say's Law, he argued, does not hold in a monetary economy because supply does not create its demand, and the latter may be insufficient to use the full capacity of the economy. In this situation, it needs macroeconomic stimulation by fiscal or monetary policy to improve the economic situation and achieve maximum welfare.

It is important to note that "A monetary economy, we shall find, is essentially one in which changing views about the future are capable of influencing the quantity of employment and not merely its direction" (Keynes 1936: XXII).[7] Changing views and expectations about the future affect today's economic consumption, investment, and savings decisions, which, in turn, determine today's effective demand. These expectations cannot be *rational* and based on *cold calculations* because the future is uncertain, not risky. Recognizing time and expectations as the basis for decisions allows for endogenous instability of markets in the monetary *economy we live in*. "He woke the Sleeping Princess from the long oblivion to which 'equilibrium' and 'perfect foresight' had condemned her and led her out into the world here and now" (Robinson 1962: 73).

Keynes' *General Theory* was indeed revolutionary, challenging the fundamentals of the neoclassical model, ranging from *models of men* to *models of markets*, from individual behavior to the functioning of markets. Keynes emphasized that economic theory helpful in developing economic policy needs to relate to *the economy we live in*. Policies relying on a theory based on overly idealized and false axioms, may be extremely costly and harmful. Awkwardly, the *General Equilibrium Model*, with its specific assumptions, often serves as the reference, even among those who favor alternative approaches. Thus, Keynes' methodological contribution to economic theory required a realistic economic theory based on real science rather than a logical science approach.

Keynes wrote the *General Theory* to chiefly address his fellow economists, igniting a tsunami of reviews of prominent economists within months after publication. The *Quarterly Journal of Economics* published

---

[6]   Some commentators argue that underemployment (involuntary unemployment) cannot be an equilibrium but that disequilibrium is a better wording but would require a dynamic analysis (Leontief 1947, Rothschild 1981). For reasons to be explained later, we use equilibrium also for nonoptimal situations.

[7]   Keynes, Preface to the General Theory, written on December 13, 1935 (Keynes 1936).

four reviews in November 1936 (by Leontief, Taussig, Robertson, and Viner). Other reviews appeared in the same year in the *Journal of Political Economy* (Hansen), *Econometrica* (Harrod), the *International Labour Review* (Lerner 1936), the *Economic Journal* (Hicks), and others.[8] The "difficulty in escaping old ideas" is arguably well illustrated in these early reviews. Many authors were struggling to grasp what Keynes possibly meant and interpreted the new theory with reference to, or even in, the framework of the neoclassical theory. Keynes' microeconomic behavioral considerations were almost totally ignored or simply turned into price rigidities. Leontief's review (1936) is sympathetic with Keynes' approach and mentions that the general equilibrium of the neoclassical model breaks down if only a few elements (persons or firms) show non-neutrality to money. A steady equilibrium requires instantaneous price reactions, and delays may cause dynamics that may not necessarily lead back to equilibrium (see also Leontief 1934, Kaldor 1934).[9]

Viner's remarks on the *General Theory* got most space in Keynes' 1937 reply "The General Theory of Employment" to the four reviews published in the *Quarterly Journal*, and he used it to sharpen his arguments. Thinking in terms of maximization and the axiomatic, logical approach to economics is most pronounced in Viner's critique. Keynes' behavioral explanations of wage and price rigidities are ignored, and he identifies as "The only clash here between Keynes' position and the orthodox one is in his denial that reduction of money wage rates is a remedy for unemployment" (Viner 1936: 237), which he relates on a short-term delay in adjustments to the new real values; just the reason Leontief put forward to deny the applicability of equilibrium analysis. People save for future consumption, hoarding (Viner 1936), stocking (Robertson 1936) are part of intertemporal maximization; savings and investments are balanced by variations of the interest rate; uncertainty and precautious saving are ignored. In his reply, Keynes (1937) emphasizes that

> [...], aggregate output depends on the propensity to hoard, on the policy of the monetary authority as it affects the quantity of money, on the state of confidence concerning the prospective yield of capital assets, on the propensity to

---

[8]   For a collection of reviews see Lekachman (1964).

[9]   In cob-web models, a time lag between demand signals and supply responses can result in convergence to, fluctuation around, and divergence from, equilibrium depending on the slopes of the demand and supply functions.

spend and on the social factors which influence the level of the money-wage. (221)

Adding that investment is severely "[…] influenced by our views of the future which we know so little" (221). Thus, Keynes emphasizes the interrelationships in the economy and uncertainty, which do not allow for a rational calculation or intertemporal maximization of hoarding and stocking. He clarifies his position on how economic theory needs to relate to *the world we live in*.

Lerner's review (1936) intended to make the *General Theory* accessible to a broader audience and focuses on the labor market. Lerner refers to Chapter 19 of the *General Theory*, where Keynes explains that nominal wage reductions will not result in proportional real wage reductions because prices will adjust with costs (wages) in the neoclassical framework. Lerner also discusses the effect of savings on aggregate demand, which may result in the adjustment of production to the lower demand, that is, the quantity (instead of prices) adjusts to equalize demand and supply (see also Howitt 1986). Harrod (1937) emphasizes the role of expectations in the *General Theory* and the resulting range of equilibrium positions. "I suggest that the most important single point in Mr. Keynes' analysis is the view that it is illegitimate to assume that the level of income in the community is independent of investment decided upon" (76). "The amount of saving depends not only on the rate of interest but on the level of income in the community" (77). Contracts are fixed in money terms (80). His only criticism (he writes) is that Keynes' theory is still static, which led Harrod to develop his growth model as a balance on the knife's edge (see Harrod 1939, Domar 1946).

Hansen (1936), later often classified as the "American Keynes," is a skeptic and concludes in his 21-page review that the *General Theory* is not a "[…] foundation stone upon which a science can be built" (686). However, he emphasizes Keynes' range of suboptimal equilibria because aggregate savings may exceed desired investments and emphasizes the role of expectations in an uncertain world: "The current consumption and investment is largely determined by anticipations of the future, by the state of optimism or pessimism" (Hansen 1936: 674). Hansen's review is one of the few which emphasizes the underlying behavioral foundations of Keynes' *General Theory*:

> The ultimate causal forces are therefore found outside the price system, in the mores, customs, habits, and behavior patterns of the people. […]

Psychological propensities, more, and behavior patterns are thus the root forces which lie back of and control consumption and investment and thereby determine what the point of equilibrium shall be. (671)

The most influential contribution still framing the interpretation of the *General Theory* is Hicks' (1937) "Mr. Keynes and the 'classics': a suggested interpretation" in which he transforms the General Theory in "Mr. Keynes' special theory" (152). Earlier Hicks regarded the "method of expectations" as "perhaps the most revolutionary thing about this book" (Hicks 1936: 239), but then he seems to neglect its consequences, arguing that Keynes' method "[…] reintroduces determinateness into a process of change … once people's expectations of future market conditions are given too" (Hicks 1936: 241). Well, at some point, decisions are made, and expectations are past, but Hicks explains that he distinguishes himself from Keynes only concerning the length of the period in which expectations are still expectations. In "IS-LM: an explanation," Hicks (1980) states that as time went by, he became dissatisfied with his original IS-LM model and emphasized that expectations affect the current period and admits that he assumed an "ultra-short-period" (141) and that, in addition, his was a full employment, flex-price model. "Neither of us [Keynes and Hicks] made any assumption about "rational expectations"; expectations in our models were strictly exogenous"(140). The motivation for liquidity preference–uncertainty–was scrapped and was simply made another "odd" price rigidity. Hicks reduced Keynes' *General Theory* to a "special case"—"depression economics"—where an increase in demand (a shift of the IS curve) will not affect the interest rate (the flat part of the LM-function).

The focus of the reviews is mainly on the macroeconomic consequences of the *General Theory* (and here, first of all, the ability of the interest mechanism to equilibrate investments and savings) and almost entirely ignoring Keynes' microfoundations which are in fundamental contrast to the neoclassical axioms. Actually, Keynes deviates from neoclassical economics in his models of humans and markets. He did not fully develop his microeconomics, but the *General Theory* is full of microfoundations (Hahn 1977) derived from observations of economic behavior in *the world we live in,* rather than being deduced from *axioms*. This is the basis of Keynes' macroeconomic conclusions. The microeconomics of Keynes' revolution was simply ignored or declared to be for exceptional cases, anomalies, money illusions, or entirely irrational.

1.4   THE NEOCLASSICAL COUNTERREVOLUTION

Reducing Keynes' theory to pure macroeconomics and aggregate relationships while ignoring his microfoundations planted the seeds for the neoclassical counterrevolution. The old way of thinking dismissed and neglected Keynes' microeconomic reasoning and made his macro conclusions a special case (i.e., *fixed price economics*) of the neoclassical model. Of course, if the price mechanism cannot guide the *invisible hand*, so the argument goes, markets cannot clear, and the economy cannot achieve the welfare optimum (the full employment equilibrium). The counterrevolution emerged in full force with the return to neoclassical *unique equilibrium economics* following Phelps' (1967, 1968) and Friedman's (1968) papers on the *natural rate of unemployment* and Lucas' assumption of *rational expectations*.[10] The simultaneous occurrence of inflation and stagnation (so-called stagflation) in the 1970s seemed to support the allegations that Keynes' (macro-) theory is *intellectually flawed* because it misses neoclassical *microfoundations* (Lucas & Sargent 1979). This allegation is without substance. Keynes' theory dismisses neoclassical axioms, but it does not miss microeconomics. In the neoclassical model, the economy achieves the welfare optimum because of carefully constructed assumptions of individual behavior and the economic environment. It is an artificial world. Nevertheless, the exceptional case of the neoclassical model became the reference in the form of the *natural rate of unemployment*.

After the neoclassical counterrevolution in the 1970s/1980s, fiscal and monetary macroeconomic policy was declared ineffective. It stimulates inflation but not production and employment. Consequently, the neoliberal counterrevolution came into full swing in the UK and US in the 1980s after Thatcher and Reagan took office. Full employment was now defined as the *natural rate of unemployment* or its companion (Eisner 1994), the NAIRU (Non-Accelerating Rate of Unemployment). Unemployment was again an equilibrium phenomenon, the result of choice, given the institutional environment. Thus, reducing unemployment required a lower *natural rate of unemployment* — a change in the incentive structure to shift the choice away from unemployment to

---

[10]   "Rational expectations" and general equilibrium is the apotheosis of neoclassical economics (Schulmeister 2018).

work. Unemployment in Europe, remaining high after every recession, was interpreted as *Eurosclerosis*, as caused by overly generous welfare states destroying the incentive to work. But this claim ignores the impact of tight fiscal and monetary policies in Europe, which caused hysteresis (Schettkat & Sun 2009). In estimates lagged unemployment contributes to explain current unemployment, which is hysteresis. "The lag interpretation says that there is yet another way to bring down the currently effective 'natural rate': just have low unemployment for a while" (Solow 1985: S33).

Neoclassical economic policy claims that unfettered markets will achieve the welfare optimum, that is, the full employment equilibrium, based on the extreme assumptions of individual behaviors and the functioning of the market. The aggregation of micro-actions to the macro-level (exemplified in *New Macroeconomics*) is achieved under the independence assumption, the independence of the individual utility functions allowing the use of the *representative agent* (averages) and simple addition. The macroeconomic outcome is x-times the micro-unit's behavior, which is deducted from the well-defined, fixed, and stable preferences determined in social isolation (i.e., ignoring social interactions through fashions, trends, and herd behavior is certainly not descriptive of *the world we live in*). Social norms are clearly relevant in labor markets (Solow 1990) but also in financial markets (arguably the closest of all markets to the "perfect market" model, Schettkat 2010); it has long been recognized that individual expectations are interdependent and are affected by the moods that Keynes' *beauty contest* emphasized.[11] "He [Keynes] was a true forerunner of behavioral finance" (Thaler 2015: 209).

1.5   BEHAVIORAL ECONOMICS: SEEDS OF THE NEXT REVOLUTION?

The distance between the neoclassical axioms from actual human economic behavior always led to deviating views among economists, as exemplified in Veblen, Simon, and Keynes' works. Even Adam Smith, to whom the "three Bs"—the Butcher, the Brewer, the Baker (Duflo & Banerjee 2019)—are ascribed, has been identified as a behavioral econ-

---

[11]   The late Minsky (1977) emphasized the endogenous instability of financial markets but he received only limited attention (see Kindleberger 1978).

omist (Ashraf, Camerer & Loewenstein 2005). In *The Theory of Moral Sentiments* (Smith 1759), published before *The Wealth of Nations* (Smith 1776), Smith dealt with issues like self-control, intertemporal choice, fairness, and altruism, all topics prominent in present Behavioral Economics. Therefore, more realistic behavioral approaches have a long tradition in economics. However, "old" Behavioral Economics is sometimes identified with Simon's work (Sent 2004), which is an essential part of Behavioral Economics, but it is undoubtedly not its beginning. The recent rising acceptance of "new" Behavioral Economics, it is argued, rests on the acceptance of the maximization of subjective expected utility (SEU). In contrast, Simon's Bounded Rationality ("old" Behavioral Economics) emphasized the restrictions for utility and profit maximization (Sent 2004). This view is not shared in this book; instead, the recent success of Behavioral Economics seems to rest on the overwhelming evidence that the neoclassical axioms are invalid as a description of actual human behavior; in fact, almost every study contradicts the assumptions.

Behavioral Economics aims to describe actual human behavior and develop an alternative to the overly abstract, unrealistic assumptions of *homo oeconomicus* by integrating insights from other disciplines (e.g., psychological, cognitive, and emotional factors). It aims to understand better how humans decide and test the neoclassical axioms and almost always neglects their validity. Behavioral Economics has discovered many regularities of individual economic behavior, which are not *rational* (*logical*, as Keynes put it) and almost always contradict the behavior deduced from the neoclassical axioms. Experiments are the dominant method and probably the reason for its recent success, but a typical response to experimental findings by *Mr. Logic* (Ariely 2008) is that these are discoveries of small-scale mistakes; interesting anecdotes. For example, Hirshleifer and Riley (1992), in their book *The Analytics of Uncertainty and Information*, first of all disregard the most critical aspect of time, which distinguishes uncertainty from risk and argue that Ellsberg's (1961) experiment on the so-called Savage's axiom (consistent subjective probability) simply

> ... illustrates certain limitations of the human mind as a computer. It is possible to fool the brain by the way a question is posed, just as optical illusions may be arranged to fool the eye. Discovering and classifying such mental illusions are fruitful activities for psychologists, but these paradoxes are of relatively little significance for economics. (Hirshleifer & Riley 1992: 34)

This statement illustrates the fundamental difference in the methodological approaches: the axiomatic approach of neoclassical economics emphasizes internal consistency vs. the approach of real science requiring descriptive content (see section 2.1). For some researchers, economics is a logical science ("Mr. Logic") where behavior can be deduced from some core principles. That is, it follows a normative approach.

Berg and Gigerenzer (2010) argue that Behavioral Economics is neoclassical economics in disguise because some Behavioral Economics contributions assume the individual's intention to maximize (i.e., to choose rationally) but are only hindered by error. They cannot discover probabilities to fully understand the relations necessary for optimizing. There are arguably two lines of research in Behavioral Economics: one assumes that people intend to maximize but are not always able to undertake the "right" decisions. Probably best illustrated with what Thaler said to Barro: "I said that the difference in our models was that he assumed that the agents in his model were as smart as he was, and I assume they were as dumb as I am. Barro agreed" (Thaler 2015: 97). Thus, Thaler assumes that people could in principle maximize but fail because of limited efforts or limited intelligence to do so. Another line in Behavioral Economics, however, assumes that the intention of individuals to maximize is limited (interview with Frank in *Challenge* 2008). Maximizing an enhanced utility function which may include a set of variables for a broader motivation such as fairness, reciprocity, or market share, image and product quality in the firms' objective function results in an even more complex optimization problem. It is a revision of the neoclassical model (Schettkat 2018a), neoclassical repairs rather than a departure from the maximizing assumption and openness to fundamentally different motivations like satisfying (Güth 2008). "Repairing the *homo oeconomicus* model means adjusting it in a way that renders observed behavior optimal" (Güth 2008: 245, emphasized in original).

Over the last decades, Behavioral Economics achieved wide acceptance and coexisted with the neoclassical model. A breakthrough was achieved when psychologists and economists began to investigate the neoclassical model's axioms in experiments, which is the core of present Behavioral Economics. Most, if not all, findings of Behavioral Economics are incompatible with neoclassical assumptions and may therefore be regarded as seeds for a new revolution in economics. However, some behavioral economists are reluctant to present their findings as an alternative model and classify it as an enrichment. For example, extending utility functions with additional variables can align with the maximization axiom but it requires an even more complex decision process. However, except for extended utility functions, almost all findings investigating behavior along the neoclassical axioms contradict the axioms. Therefore, the evidence suggests that Behavioral Economics is an alternative rather than a revision of the neoclassical model (Schettkat 2018a).

Even if the fundamentals, or axioms, of the neoclassical model are contradicted, the theory may still be used to build models within this framework. They describe *life* in the artificial world, not *in the economy we live in*. Thus, policies deduced from the model can hardly be applied to our world. Behavioral Economics is not a consistently designed model, nor does it predict uniform economic behavior. However, its findings may serve as the seeds of a shift away from the neoclassical paradigm (as Kuhn (1970) described it).[12] Keynes' microeconomics is very well supported by the behavioral economic findings of this argument. Behavioral Economics is not limited to those authors who classify themselves under this label in this book. Instead, the term is used *broadly* and includes theories that integrate actual human behavior, including concepts such as framing, bounded rationality, norms, socially embedded individuals and their interactions, routines, and heuristics.

1.6   MODELS OF HUMANS AND MODELS OF MARKETS

Keynes' theory and Behavioral Economics both require economic theory to be descriptive. It should not contradict actual economic behavior. This distinguishes them from the neoclassical model, which deduces economic behavior from the *first principles* and the *axioms* about human intentions and behavior. Most *Behavioral Economic studies* focus on individual behavior (models of humans). It is here where Behavioral Economics and Keynes' theory can be regarded as congruent. Keynes and some behavioral economists (e.g., Akerlof 2002, 2007, Akerlof & Shiller 2009, de Grauwe 2011, 2012) made the second step. They analyzed the macroeconomic consequences of the microfoundations on the functioning of markets (models of markets), challenging the perfect

---

[12]   Johnson (1971) argued that a vulnerable dominant theory which can be blamed for policy failures together with novel conclusions may cause a "revolution." For a discussion of whether or not Behavioral Economics is an extension or an alternative of the neoclassical approach and whether it is a *Revision or Revolution* see Schettkat (2018a).

market model of neoclassical economics. Keynes based his microfoundation on *casual* observations of economic behavior in *the world we live in*. Behavioral Economics made a much more systematic effort to establish evidence on actual microeconomic behavior. The basis of applicable economic policies requires being descriptive rather than abstracting from actual economic behavior. Description, rather than prescription, is the big methodological difference between Keynes and Behavioral Economics, on the one hand, and the axiomatic neoclassical approach, on the other. The neoclassical axioms are extreme assumptions or very special case. Keynes clearly warned researchers not to derive economic policy proposals from overly idealized, abstract neoclassical axioms just on the first page of Chapter 1 of the *General Theory* (Keynes 1936: 3): "Moreover, the characteristics of the special case assumed by the classical theory happen not to be those of the economic society in which we actually live, with the result that its teaching is misleading and disastrous if we attempt to apply it to the facts of experience." The sophisticated and careful experiments and tests in Behavioral Economics extend far beyond Keynes' *casual* observations of individual economic behavior and provide rigorous evidence for regularities in economic human behavior, which contradict neoclassical axioms that cannot be ignored anymore and may provide the seeds for a more realistic economics (see Table 1.1 for a summary).

Keynes and Behavioral Economics deviate from neoclassical economics concerning the individual's motivation and ability to maximize utility and profits (i.e., choosing among the myriad of alternatives that provide the highest utility, profit, respectively). The meso- and macroeconomic consequences from this rejection of the neoclassical axioms are less developed in Behavioral Economics, although not entirely absent. Keynes also challenged the *General Equilibrium* model concerning the market processes based on his microfoundations (see for a summary Table 1.2). *The world we live in* is not risky, where one can meaningfully compute expected values. Instead, it is uncertain.

The economy is not static. It does not move along a steady-state path that is only pushed out of equilibrium by occasional external shocks following a known probability distribution; markets are endogenously unstable. The axioms and auxiliary assumptions of the neoclassical model led to the postulate that markets are stable and achieve an equilibrium quickly, or at least in the long run. Hence, the actual market processes may be irrelevant. One may analyze the economy as jumping from one equilibrium to another, as in *comparative statics* where the

Table 1.1   *Models of humans: Keynes and Behavioral Economics vs. neoclassical*

Commonalities Between Keynes' Theory and Behavioral Economics	Neoclassical Assumptions
Methodology (Real Science vs. Logical Science)	
Inductive, socially embedded, descriptive (*the world we live in*)	Axiomatic, deductive, prescriptive, individualistic
Methods Building the Knowledge Base	
Observations, interviews, experiments, neurological analysis	Axioms
Motivation of Economic Agents	
Broad, not necessarily maximization, satiation	Narrow, maximization
Context, Mental State, Mood, Animal Spirits, Emotions	
Important, influences decisions	Irrelevant
Preferences	
Dynamic, depending on reference points (e.g., societal, groups, previous experience), habituation, interdependent, social interactions	Stable, ordered, individualistic, independent (socially isolated)
Perception of the Economy (the World)	
Maybe biased (the map is not the territory), framing matters (the way choices are expressed affects decisions)	Unbiased
Magnitudes, Monetary Values	
Influential, important, orientation, reference points, not neutral	Irrelevant, only real values and relative prices matter, neutral
Rationality	
Imperfect, non-rational heuristics, routines, animal spirits	Perfect
Expectations	
Non-rational	Rational
Computational Ability ("RAM")	
Limited	High (unlimited)
Self-Control	
Imperfect, limited	Perfect
Social Status	
Important, socially integrated individuals	Irrelevant
Fairness, Justice, Distribution, Norms	
Important may overrule material interests	Unimportant
Unemployment	
Not utility-maximizing choice, individual disequilibrium, overwhelmingly involuntary, quantity constraint	Utility-maximizing choice, individual optimum (voluntary)
Work	
Provides income but also direct utility (enjoying doing)	Provides no direct utility

sequence of events is irrelevant and time is not essential (i.e., the market system is assumed to be ergodic, dominated by negative feedback effects). No matter what happens in between, the economy will settle at the unique equilibrium (i.e., the optimum). The economy is in a static or a steady-state equilibrium.

In *the economy we live in*, time is critical. Today's decisions depend on the expectations of tomorrow's demand affecting today's production and employment. Economic decisions are forward-looking, based on expectations in an uncertain environment, and arguably the most important concept of the *General Theory*. These expectations cannot be rational or risky. They suffer from uncertainty because economic development is endogenous. Interactions among economic agents may result in positive feedback effects. Consequently, expectations cannot be based on *cold calculations*; they cannot be *rational expectations*. Even if the economy tends to a equilibrium, this equilibrium is not unique. Instead, it is endogenously determined in a dynamic economy (Schumpeter 1911).

Variations in expectations affect the economic future, resulting in many different equilibria and not in the unique equilibrium of full employment of the neoclassical model. Keynes' new theory was difficult to reconcile with the old beliefs and doctrines. It questioned several core pillars of neoclassical economics, shaking up the General Equilibrium model's carefully refined theoretical architecture or superstructure. Leaving old ideas and beliefs behind with which he and his fellow economists grew up is more complicated than creating new ideas, Keynes (1936) discovered.

1.7   THIS BOOK

Theories and models frame our thinking. They shape the space of opportunities for what seems plausible, what we regard as reasonable, and what we discard as illusionary, impossible, or even crazy. The space of opportunities for thinking is defined by fundamental assumptions made to build up our theories, determining our frame of thinking. This book argues that Keynes' revolutionary macroeconomic consequences are based on his microeconomic foundations derived from observations of economic behavior and conditions of *the world we live in,* which are no less revolutionary than his macroeconomics compared. The macroeconomic predictions of the neoclassical model, single equilibrium at the optimum (full employment), and *General Equilibrium* are deduced from the neoclassical axioms of rational economic behavior and the assumed

Table 1.2   *Market models, Keynes and Behavioral Economics vs.*
                 neoclassical

Commonalities Between Keynes' Theory and Behavioral Economics	Neoclassical Assumptions
Equilibrium	
Multiple can be suboptimal, below full employment, no automatic tendency to optimum	Unique, optimum, automatic movement to optimum
Stability of Markets	
Endogenous instability (expectations), dynamic	Stable, static (steady states), disturbed by external shocks
Feedback Effects	
Can be positive (fashion, trends, income), nonergodic processes included	Negative, ergodic system
Monetary	
Money has several functions (transactions, liquidity, precautionary savings)	Money is a veil
Monetary policy affects the real economy (production, employment)	Monetary policy does not affect the real economy
Probability Distribution of Future Events	
Mostly unknown (uncertainty)	Known (risk)
Representative Agent	
Not applicable, heterogeneity	Applicable
Time	
Historical, expectations, sequential, path dependence, non-ergodic	Logical (ergodic) rational expectations
Asymmetric (economy may change and may not return to former equilibrium)	symmetric responses (return to equilibrium)
Adjustment Mechanisms	
Prices and quantities, imperfect information, no auctioneer, trade at non-equilibrium prices possible	Prices (equilibrium prices)
Regulation (rules)	
May stabilize markets	Disturbing otherwise stable markets

conditions. They rest on the axioms claimed to be obvious and thus, do not need any justification.[13] In actuality, these axioms are at odds with *the economy we live in* and are strongly substantiated by the findings of Behavioral Economics and Keynes' observations. Deviations from *rationality* (utility and profit-maximizing) are often labeled *irrational, paradoxes,* meaning at odds with the maximization hypothesis. Given the astonishing neoclassical axioms it is the more surprising that they remained the yardstick for good economic theory, and anything else was classified as laymen's economics or even intellectually flawed (Lucas & Sargent 1979).

For a long time, macroeconomics was Keynesian, while microeconomics remained neoclassical, often labeled schizophrenia, indicating the contradictory coexistence. However, the experiments and tests in Behavioral Economics, extending far beyond Keynes' "casual" observations, provide rigorous evidence for regularities in human economic behavior, which are, to an astonishing degree, comparable, if not congruent, with Keynes' observations: Humans are socially embedded instead of isolated. They care about fairness, distribution, and status. Their preferences are dynamic and depend on reference points. Large parts of the Behavioral Economics literature are concerned with individual behavior (micro). Keynes also analyzed the consequences of actual human economic decision-making for markets and the macroeconomy.

Chapter 2 discusses *fundamentals*: The core questions include (a) whether or not economics is a logical or real science, (b) whether a model deduced from axioms (the neoclassical model) is sufficient to understand the economy, and (c) whether or not economic theory needs to relate to actual economic behavior, as required in Behavioral Economics and Keynes' theory (2.1). The answers to these questions lead directly to discussing the different methods to build the knowledge base (2.2), such as observations, experiments, interviews etc. The rationality concept, that is, maximizing, is discussed in section 2.3. The fundamental differences between Keynes' multiple equilibria, which are balances of forces without any notion to their quality, and the neoclassical optimal and unique equilibrium concept are clarified in section

---

[13] Merriam-Webster explains that an axiom is self-evidently true; hence, it does not require proof. Therefore, it is surprising that the neoclassical axioms survived as the basis for *good economic theory*. The neoclassical axioms, however, are not self-evident, and even those who regard neoclassical axioms as the sine qua non, usually admit that individuals do not behave according to the axioms.

2.4. Another fundamental question is whether or not microeconomics is needed to understand macroeconomics. The aggregation problem aside, it is argued here that the General Equilibrium Model relies on its very specific neoclassical assumptions. Relaxing the strict neoclassical assumptions and applying descriptive behavioral microfoundations will result in different macroeconomic outcomes as Keynes demonstrated in the *General Theory* (2.5). The equilibrium concepts and the economy's nature as static (steady) predictable and inherently stable versus dynamic and endogenously unstable affect the critical distinction between risk and uncertainty, between foresight and the unforeseeable future. Do we live in an economy which is risky and meaningful probabilities can be applied to calculate outcomes or is the economic future uncertain and depending on our decisions (2.6). From the individuals' perspective, this comes down to whether they understand the whole (complex and dynamic) economy and use this information to determine their optimal plans or whether they face cognitive limitations preventing rational choice even if intended. The market clears by price variations which seems quite logical on the basis of the market diagram with well-ordered supply and demand functions but if the functions are unknown, the outcome may be different. The pioneer of experiments in economics, Chamberlin (1948), showed that in markets without an auctioneer, non-renegotiations of prices and sequential decisions, the equilibrium may not be achieved (2.7).

Chapter 3 investigates the concepts and preconditions for maximization (rational choice), which depends on the significant preconditions usually not fulfilled, that is that rational choice is a normative and not a descriptive concept. For ordinary persons not trained in neoclassical economics, deciding rationally simply means behaving purposefully, considering some pros and cons when deciding upon more significant purchases. However, in economics, deciding rationally requires choosing the best, utility-maximizing, profit-maximizing option among the innumerous alternatives. Information about all the other options and their evaluation must be available. The decision context must be clear and understood, unbiased etc. Behavior deviating from normative rationality is often—even among those critical about the rationality assumptions— classified as irrational, an anomaly, a paradox, or simply declared irrelevant and ignored. However, there are many deviations from rationality occurring even among the champions of decision theory (see Chapter 3) as Allais (1953) has demonstrated. Using *rational choice* as the yardstick turns the world upside down, given the rationality axioms' very restrictive assumptions and normative characteristics. Critiques argue that the decision concept needs to be descriptive rather than prescriptive. The findings in Behavioral Economics clearly show that framing affects decisions. The choice environment is often complex, expected, and experienced. Utility may differ. The transitivity condition is impossible to fulfill, and preferences change. The necessary information for maximization cannot be processed.

Decisions are future-oriented and thus, depending on expectations and uncertainty rather than risk may lead to different decisions (Chapter 4). Rational choice requires a clear ranking of the outcomes of all options but under uncertainty probability distributions are simply unknown preventing calculations. How to decide under uncertainty? Keynes argued that after weighting pros and cons the last kick in a decision depends on emotions, animal spirits, which is unacceptable among the rational choice theorists. Recent progress in neurological research, however, demonstrates that decisions require emotions, animal spirits.

Neoclassical economics abstracts from time, but its impact on expectations is profound (Chapter 5). Preferences are simply assumed to be predetermined, stable, and independent of today's and past actions. Actually, the economic environment may change, the expected utility (profit) and experienced utility (profit) may differ, current decisions may affect future choices, and we may develop habits affecting our future behavior. The *rational expectations* revolution primarily connected with Lucas' work rests on the assumption of a predictable economic environment with stochastic deviations around an equilibrium or an equilibrium path. The economy is assumed to be essentially static (or, for that matter, following a steady-state), a stochastic version of perfect foresight, as Arrow put it. Lucas was prepared to limit his reasoning to the stable, static world, but that is not *the world we live in.* Behavioral Economics shows that history matters and that so-called reference points affect utilities. For *rational choices* today, future payments need to be transformed into present values using discounting. However, it turns out that amounts and nominal values influence decisions. Large sums are discounted at lower rates, and over time the discounting functions seem hyperbolic and irrational but common.

Chapter 6 focuses on the consequences of analyzing socially embedded individuals instead of individuals forming their preferences in isolation. On the first pages of the *General Theory,* Keynes rejected "utility maximization," arguing that the neoclassical postulate that the real wage equals the marginal disutility of work is false. The findings in Behavioral Economics confirm Keynes' observations. Workers resist nominal wage reductions but do not react immediately to a decline in real wages. Workers care about relative wages and try to control their social position referenced by the nominal wage.[14] Social positions, however, are incompatible with the forming of preferences in social isolation and the balancing of the marginal utility of leisure against the disutility of working for an income in real terms (goods). For neoclassical economists trained to think in models of socially isolated individuals, where money is a veil covering the real wages, the nominal wage orientation is simply "irrational." Moreover, since *homo oeconomicus* is assumed to be rational, i.e., maximizing real variables and interpreting the world without bias, they turned nominal wage resistance into a *money illusion*. A wording which suggests a mistake but it exists. In neoclassical theory, money is just a veil covering the real values, the classical dichotomy.[15] Whether rational or not, Keynes and Behavioral Economics require that

---

[14]   The resistance to nominal wage cuts but accepting real wage reductions through inflation is probably the least well understood element in Keynes' theory because many economists are so much used to think of independent, socially isolated individuals maximizing their utility depending on goods rather than relative positions and regarding institutional arrangements as disturbances of the assumed perfectly working Walrasian General Equilibrium Model. Resistance to nominal wage cuts then simply becomes price rigidity, fixed prices and, of course, markets cannot clear with fixed prices. Leijonhufvud (1967: 402) refers to Patinkin (1948) who argues "[…] that, to Keynes, rigidity was a policy recommendation and not a behavioral assumption." Indeed, Keynes (1936) concluded that downward flexible (nominal) wages will probably not achieve higher employment but may rather reduce it further due to declining demand. But Keynes took the resistance to nominal wage cuts as a fact based on his observations. The Leijonhufvud and Patinkin argument shows the affinity to logic rather than actual human behavior.

By contrast, Hirschman argues that given the myriad of assumptions underlying the neoclassical model, the claim "that we have to deal with men and women, or with groups thereof, 'as they really are' […]" (Hirschman 1992: 45). "The mixture of paradoxical insight and alchemy involved in these constructs make them powerfully attractive, but also account for their ultimate vulnerability" (Hirschman 1992: 45). Why buy a sportscar if you just want to get from A to B, speed limits restrict driving and you are forming your preferences in isolation? However, many items we purchase are actually "positional goods" (Hirsch 1976) deriving their usefulness from scarcity.

[15]   Whether money illusion or not, the assumption in neoclassical economics is that downward flexible wages will lead to equilibrium in the labor market. Hahn and Solow (1986) asked the blasphemous question "Is wage flexibility a good thing?" and comment that economics is not a religion and refer to Chapter 19 of the *General Theory* (see below).

economic theory needs to be based on assumptions relating to *the world we live in*, or at least not contrary to it.

The rise and fall of unique-equilibrium economics and the theoretical foundations of the neoliberal model's revitalization, based on neoclassical theory, are analyzed in Chapter 7. It was the neoclassical counterrevolution hitting Keynesianism hard because it was equated to the Phillips tradeoff between inflation and unemployment, which is incompatible with the neoclassical model in which monetary values (nominal wages) can, if at all, only briefly affect production and employment. Phelps and Friedman argued that macroeconomic policy could not affect the tradeoff because the economy returns to its unique equilibrium, the *natural rate of unemployment* (the NAIRU, respectively), in the long run, or according to the *rational expectations hypothesis* even in the short run.

Unemployment was again the result of choice, resulting from individual utility maximization within the given institutional framework (i.e., incentive structure). Labor markets clear at the *natural rate of unemployment*. The models predict that stimulating macroeconomic policy is ineffective for production and employment. It will only result in higher prices and inflation rates. The 1970s experienced rising inflation with high unemployment (stagflation). Since the *natural rate theory* was developed before stagflation (in the 1960s), it was praised as a *theory ahead of the facts* (Blanchard 1997). The *natural rate of unemployment* became the definition of *full employment*, the optimal use of resources in the current incentive structure, and guided economic policy among conservative and even social-democratic politicians. This is a first-class example of how economic theory frames thinking and determines the room for economic possibilities. However, where is the *natural rate*? Observations and estimations show that it varies with time and jumps around. Recent developments show very low inflation rates with widely different unemployment rates suggesting that the industrialized economies are less confronted with unemployment regimes. Instead, various unemployment rates can occur with similar inflation rates.

The book concludes (Chapter 8) with a plea for an economic theory that aligns with *the world we live in* and does not contradict actual human behavior. Our imagination of economic theory determines what our economic possibilities allow for. Suppose economic models are overly abstract and out of touch with *the economy we live in*. If this is the case, the imminent risk of an axiomatic approach or policy conclusion and prescriptions may be useless or even harmful.

2. Fundamentals of economics

Understanding our overly complex economy requires simplifications and generalizations to guide our thinking and conclusions; in other words, it needs a theory. "All theory depends on assumptions which are not quite true. That is what makes it theory" (Solow 1956: 65). Which simplifications and generalizations can be made without determining the outcome? How do we distinguish the important from the less relevant? Theory guides our economic thinking in the right or the wrong direction; it can work as glasses helping to understand the possibilities and restrictions of economic policy. It may also place false limits on our economic prospects. The fundamental assumptions, the premises, and *axioms* represent our knowledge base and determine our conclusions as Ramsey—referring to Kant, Wittgenstein, De Morgan, and Pierce—wrote:

> All these authors agree that the conclusion of a formally valid argument is contained in its premisses; that to deny the conclusion while accepting the premisses would be self-contradictory; that a formal deduction does not increase our knowledge, but only brings out clearly what we already know in another form; and that we are bound to accept its validity on pain of being inconsistent with ourselves. The logical relation which justifies the inference is that the sense or import of the conclusion is contained in that of the premisses. (1926: 185–186)

Logical deductions follow once the premises, the fundamental assumptions, or axioms are accepted. The axioms determine the conclusions. Therefore it is of utmost importance how the basic knowledge is generated. This chapter sets the stage for the most relevant fundamentals, of which some will be discussed in more depth and illustrated in the later chapters.

Keynes and Behavioral Economics contrast with the neoclassical model on several points. Above all, the methodological approach (see also Marglin 2018), that is, whether economics is a mathematical-logical science or a real science (section 2.1). This distinction affects the methods used to create the knowledge base (section 2.2). To choose rationally, in a calculated maximizing manner, depends on manifold preconditions for humans' motivation and abilities and the economic environment (section 2.3). Given the restrictive assumptions, it may come as a surprise that "rational choice" became the *sine qua non* of good economic theory (Akerlof & Yellen 1987). Maximization of profits and utility is the overarching goal in neoclassical economics, but utility is anything else than clearly defined (section 2.3). Equilibrium connotes harmony and balance, but it refers to totally different situations in Keynes' theory and the neoclassical general equilibrium model. In the latter, equilibrium refers to the optimum the economy is assumed to achieve automatically, but in Keynes' economics, the economy may be balanced in suboptimal situations (section 2.4), sometimes labeled "disequilibrium." The interaction among micro-units does not allow for macro-conclusions simply based on micro behavior (section 2.6).

The equilibrium concepts, the nature of the economy as timeless, static (steady) vs. historical, dynamic, affects the distinction between risk and uncertainty, between foresight and the unforeseeable future. Differences in the fundamentals lead to models of men and markets that differ sharply between Keynes' theory, Behavioral Economics on the one side, and the neoclassical model on the other. The neoclassical model deduces endogenously stable markets or quickly achieving the optimum (equilibrium), which can only be disturbed by external shocks. But the *economy we live in* is uncertain, which increases with time. Under uncertainty—rather than under risk—the outcome of decisions cannot be calculated and rational, but decisions need to be influenced by emotions, intuition, routines, heuristics, and *animal spirits*.[1]

2.1   LOGICAL OR REAL SCIENCE?

The axiomatic approach applied in mathematical and logical sciences takes certain postulates (axioms, premises) as starting points from which other relations are logically deduced. "[...] 'truth' is a logical criterion. A conclusion is 'true' if it follows from the premises through deductions which are, after all, tautological" (Kornai 1971: 8). By contrast, in the real sciences (such as physics or biology), "the only criterion of 'truth' is experience, the comparison of assertions with reality" (Kornai

---

[1]   A conundrum is the short-run vs. long-run distinction in the neoclassical synthesis, where disequilibrium may occur in the short run, but for the long run, the perfect market equilibrium is assumed (see Chapter 5).

1971: 8). Real science, of course, does not refrain from logical and mathematical reasoning (just take physics), but whether economics is a logical-mathematical science or a real one is at the core of the methodological dispute. The neoclassical model deduces economic behavior from narrow and abstract axioms, and some auxiliary assumptions (Arrow 1986) declared to be evident without further investigations; in other words, it follows the logical-mathematical approach emphasizing logical consistency with the axioms. Behavioral Economics and Keynes' theory, however, insist that economics is a *real science* where "[...] only those theorems and propositions (deduced from assumptions not in conflict with reality) which describe the real world more or less accurately may be considered acceptable" (Kornai 1971: 9).

How are the axioms representing the fundamental knowledge established?[2] "We can regard perception, memory, and induction as the three fundamental ways of acquiring knowledge; deduction, on the other hand, is merely a method of arranging our knowledge and eliminating inconsistencies or contradictions" (Ramsey 1926: 186). This also means that the knowledge base of the neoclassical model is induced from perceptions and observations. Still, it overemphasizes and generalizes a specific part of human motivation (independent individual utility maximization) as its core axiom from which economic behavior is deduced. According to Behavioral Economics, however, "[...] the realism of the psychological underpinnings of economic analysis will improve the field of economics on its own terms—generating theoretical insights, making better predictions of field phenomena, and suggesting better policy" (Camerer & Loewenstein 2004: 3).[3] Keynes also required the basic assumptions to fit *the world we live in:* "For if orthodox economics is at fault, the error is to be found not in the superstructure, which has been erected with great

---

[2]   In his Presidential address to the American Economic Association, "Science and Ideology," Schumpeter (1948) emphasized that intuition and vision motivating research is inevitability ideological but that this bias may diminish through the interaction of economists.

[3]   Camerer and Loewenstein continue that the previous statement does not imply a "[...] wholesale rejection of the neoclassical approach to economics based on utility maximization, equilibrium, and efficiency" (Camerer & Loewenstein 2004: 3). However, most findings of Behavioral Economics contradict the fundamental assumptions of the neoclassical model and are therefore better described as "revolution" rather than "revision" (Schettkat 2018a).

care for logical consistency, but in a lack of clearness and generality in the premisses" (Keynes 1936: xxi) in the axioms.

In his *Treatise on Probability* (1921), Keynes states that knowledge is always incomplete and that inductions can never be free of doubt, that is, some uncertainty[4] remains. This is also known as Popper's (1959) "Black Swan Fallacy." Inductions cannot establish the truth, but they are the major source of inspiration for the basic knowledge of economic theory. How else shall we establish hypotheses? However, one may carefully analyze the adequacy of generalizations manifested in fundamental assumptions. It is hard to see how conclusions deduced from premises contradicting actual economic behavior can lead to valid results.

Friedman (1953) argued the reverse: Theories cannot be judged by the validity of their axioms, which are instrumental and do not need proof. Theory can only be proved by comparing its predictions with observed outcomes. This is often labeled "positive economics." Friedman (1953: 8) argued even that "Truly important and significant hypotheses will be found to have 'assumptions' that are wildly inaccurate descriptive representations of reality, and, in general, the more significant the theory, the more unrealistic the assumptions (in this sense)." The less the assumptions fit actual behavior, the better the theory? "F-twist" (Samuelson 1963). Declaring fundamental assumptions to be instrumental satisfies the requirements of mathematical-logical sciences, but in real sciences, instrumentalism forces scientists to abandon the search for truth (Popper, according to Caldwell 1980: 370).

Lucas and Sargent (1978), in their fundamental attack on Keynesian economics and their plea for neoclassical microfoundations, specify *maximization* and *equilibrium* as the core axioms from which models of men and models of markets can be deduced. According to them, *maximization* and *equilibrium* constitute the knowledge base of the neoclassical model. Solow (1978) commented that maximization is empty as long as

---

[4] Keynes used "uncertainty" in his "Treatise of Probability" in an epistemological sense. He discussed philosophical approaches to probability especially concerned with the uncertainty involved in induced knowledge, which is the black swan problem (see Popper 1959 and Taleb 2007). "In other words, Pure Induction can be usefully employed to strengthen an argument, after a certain number of instances have been examined, we have, from some other source, a finite probability in favour of the generalisation [...] as to its conclusion been satisfied by the next hitherto unexamined instance which satisfies it premiss" (Keynes 1921: 238).

it is not specified what is to be maximized (see section 2.3) and that the insistence on always achieving equilibrium is simply false. Individual markets, and the macroeconomy, can be out of optimal equilibrium. When Friedman claimed that the theory's predictions are in accordance with actual outcomes, he assumed that the outcome is the optimum or full employment. But how do we know whether observed choices and situations are profit or utility maxima at the micro and macro levels? "No one has, in fact, observed whether the actual positions of business firms are the profit-maximizing ones [...]" (Simon 1963: 230) let alone utility maximization ones. Firms may lack the information they need to maximize profits (Hassink & Schettkat 2003) and Arrow (1978: 169) emphasizes the importance of quantity constraints on firms: "Indeed it would be hard otherwise to explain why firms lay off workers. Since their capital costs are sunk in the short-run, they should be prepared to sell so long as their prices cover variable costs."

Similarly, nobody has ever shown that the economy is in the optimal equilibrium; this is simply an assertion (Blinder & Solow 1973). Simon criticizes the circularity of the neoclassical approach: under the maximization assumption, observed choices are declared maximizing choices (rational choices, see section 2.3 and Chapter 3) without proof and measurement. "When verification is demanded, they [neoclassical economists] tend to look for evidence that the theory makes correct predictions and resist advice that they should look instead directly at the decision mechanisms and processes" (Simon 1986: 38). However, the knowledge base, meaning the presumptions and axioms of the neoclassical model, can be and actually are investigated in Behavioral Economics: Do people intend to maximize, what are they maximizing, and are they able to maximize? Based on the axiom of individual utility maximization, it is deduced that observed choices must be utility-maximizing. Otherwise, "rational" individuals who are "free to choose" would have decided differently. This conclusion is logically consistent but hardly proof that outcomes are utility-maximizing; it is simply deduced from the maximization axiom leaving open what utility is, let alone how it can be measured.[5] "All too often theoretical deductions are untested and/or based on untested premises. Worse yet, either the conclusions or the assumptions may be untestable" (Blinder et al. 1998: 11).

---

[5]   Utility, it is argued, is ordinal but many arguments actually rely on cardinal utility.

Neoclassical economics applies a normative approach. The intention to maximize is assumed without any further investigation. "What is really needed, in most cases, is a very difficult and seldom very neat assessment and verification of these assumptions in terms of observed facts. Here mathematics cannot help and because of this, the interest and enthusiasm of the model builder suddenly begins to flag [...]" (Leontief 1971: 2). Still, the growing non-normative approaches require direct evidence of motivation and decision processes. Do people intend to, and can they establish the transitive order of alternatives to consistent preference functions? Are the individual's preferences stable and independent from past decisions and the social environment directed by relative prices only? Or do economic agents develop customs and habits? Even if individuals intend to maximize and follow precise preference functions, can they possibly know the utility of all alternatives and proceed with the enormous amount of information? All these issues have been investigated in Behavioral Economics.

2.2 METHODS TO BUILD THE KNOWLEDGE BASE

2.2.1 Interviews

To generate a realistic, more descriptive knowledge base for economics, direct and open-minded analysis of humans' motivation and decision procedures is the explicit goal of Behavioral Economics. What is the motivation for the observed choices? Do individuals intend to maximize? If so, what are they maximizing? Where do the desires and aspirations come from? What are the influences of the social environment, advertisements, and trends? Do individuals perform the necessary evaluation of alternative choices and rank them according to expected utility? There are several ways to establish the knowledge base for microeconomic theory: observations, interviews, experiments, and neurological analysis. Keynes relied on observations and reflected on the economic circumstances (see Chapters 3 and 4). The most straightforward approach to learning about observed economic behavior's intentions and motivations is "asking those who are doing" (Blinder 1990). However, interviews are regarded with skepticism among neoclassical economists because, as the argument goes, individuals will not reveal their true motives, which is maximization by assumption. This is a surprising response, given that preferences are assumed to be formed independently from the social environment. Why then care about expressing one's motivation? Several economists did not shy away from interviews (e.g., Blinder 1991, Blinder et al. 1998, Bewley 1995, 1999, Flanagan, Strauss & Ulman 1974). Blinder et al. (1998) reminded the skeptics of the reliability of interviews and questionnaires that these instruments also generate the "hard data" commonly used in economics (such as GDP, wages, employment and unemployment statistics, inflation).

Instead of maximizing, individuals may try to achieve aspiration levels (Selten 1990), so-called satisfying (Simon 1978), rather than aiming for the unspecified maximum. This seems to guide New York cab drivers, who can freely vary their working hours and seem to stop driving once they achieve their income targets (Camerer et al. 1997). Instead of maximizing income on busy days, they are aiming at an aspiration level. New York's taxi drivers became a topic of controversy, and defenders of the maximization hypothesis put forward arguments ranging from data issues to drivers' personalities to the ease of driving under different weather conditions.

Even if individuals intend to maximize, to make "rational choices," it is open to question whether they can collect and proceed with the enormous amount of information necessary to choose the utility-maximizing alternative among the myriad of other options. Furthermore, future-oriented decisions are generally characterized by uncertainty or, at best, by probability (see section 2.5). No wonder that many analyses of rational choice use games to reduce the complexity of *the world we live in* into fixed rules, defined payments, and well-known probabilities (e.g., von Neumann and Morgenstern's (1944) influential *Theory of Games and Economic Behavior*). However, "In situations that are complex and in which information is very incomplete (i.e., virtually all real world situations), the behavioral theories deny that there is any magic for producing behavior even approximating an objective maximization of profits or utilities" (Simon 1986: 39). If humans decide *irrationally*, these decisions are classified as paradoxes or anomalies, but ignorance can hardly convince the skeptic. Critics of the rationality axiom argue that the human brain cannot collect and process the information and evaluate all possible choices, arrange them in a transitive order, and consider all consequences of specific decisions. Intended rationality is therefore bounded (Simon 1955, 1982).

Bewley (1995, 1999) argues that comparing predictions and outcomes can establish significant deviations from deduced behavioral axioms, but it cannot reveal motivations. In other words, the knowledge base remains untouched; the method does not provide any information on the motivation of observed decisions. Bewley's interview study solved an important longstanding puzzle in labor economics: why employers are reluctant to reduce their workers' (money) wages in situations of excess labor supply. He summarizes:

> However, the main causes of downward wage rigidity have to do with employers' belief that other motivators are necessary, which are best thought of as having to do with generosity. Employers want their workers to identify with the objectives of the organization and to cooperate in good spirit with coworkers and supervisors. (Bewley 1995: 252)

Thus, employers fear that "[b]ad morale may lead to lower productivity or even to carelessness verging on sabotage" (Solow 1979: 80). This is confirmed by the Krueger and Mas (2003) analysis of labor disputes at a Firestone factory, which led to a rise in defective tires.[6]

2.2.2 Observations and Experiments

Economists have long agreed that economic issues cannot be tested in controlled experiments like in the "hard sciences." The advantage of experiments is that variables and frames can be changed in a controlled way to test whether humans respond differently to variations in environmental conditions, whether they change the decision criteria, if and how they adjust discount rates based on time and magnitudes, and whether preferences remain stable over time. In short, experiments were used to evaluate the core axioms of the neoclassical model, producing no favorable news for the neoclassical axioms. The disadvantage of experiments, of course, is that people may behave one way in laboratories and another way in *the world we live in.*

V. Smith (2002a) distinguishes Experimental Economics from Behavioral Economics because, in Experimental Economics experiments, participants make "real choices" and may earn "real money," he argues.[7] In Behavioral Economics, the experiments remain (often) hypothetical without any real consequences for participants. For sure, experiments are not *the world we live in.* Still, they control some environmental variables and use, for example, medical brain scanners, which

---

6   See Kahneman, Knetsch and Thaler (1986).
7   See Riedl (2009) for a discussion.

are presumably the most reliable instruments to measure reactions, to show strong brain reactions on hypothetical changes in relative positions without any monetary consequences.

The findings of experiments in Behavioral Economics reveal that humans sometimes make "wrong" choices because they do not fully understand the situation, especially if probabilities are involved. But often, it is not the misinterpretations of situations that result in decisions deviating from *rational choice*; even after clarifications, *irrational* people insist on sticking to their *irrational* decisions. It is not simply a money illusion; when nominal values are factors in economic decisions, they can even overrule real values concerning utility.

Presumably, the first published experiments in economics were undertaken at Harvard University in the 1940s by Chamberlin (1948), who investigated whether markets converge to equilibrium. Allais (1953) and Ellsberg (1961) designed other early experiments explicitly testing neoclassical axioms. Allais found that the decision criteria changed from expected payments to higher probability, resulting in contradictory choices, known as Allais' paradox (see Chapter 3). Ellsberg (1961) tested whether participants violate "subjective expected utility" (SEU, see Chapter 4) under uncertainty in an experiment similar to Keynes' thought experiment (Keynes 1921). If the decision procedures deduced from the neoclassical axioms are not confirmed with various research methods (observations, interviews, and experiments), their validity is probably not as obvious as claimed.

2.2.3   Neurological Analysis

Neurobiologists are gradually decoding the functions of our brain with the help of functional magnetic resonance brain imaging (fMRI). They can link decision processes to specific parts of the brain. Some parts of the brain, like the amygdala (the evolutionarily oldest part of the brain), are related to emotions (Cohen 2005), while other areas, like the frontal cortex, are related to cognitive processes. Cohen (2005) argues that different parts of our brain evolved at different times, with the frontal cortex being the latest to develop. The frontal cortex distinguishes humans from other primates. "One of the most important insights of neuroscience is that the brain is not a homogenous processor, but rather involves a melting of diverse specialized processes that are integrated in different ways when the brain faces different types of problems" (Loewenstein, Rick & Cohen 2008: 649). Damásio (1994) famously showed that decisions require emotions. Cohen (2005: 3) adds: "Emotions influence our decisions. They do so in just about every walk of our lives, whether we are aware of it and whether we acknowledge it or not" (Cohen 2005: 3). However, this does not exclude cognitive processes from decision-making. It seems that emotional and cognitive areas are interacting.

Neurologists used natural experiments to test their hypotheses. They observed malfunctions in patients who had suffered from damage to specific parts of the brain. This method has been used more widely in recent years, partly in cooperation with economists (neuroeconomics), presenting arguably the hardest facts on decision processes.

> Neuroeconomics, we argue, has further bridged the once disparate fields of economics and psychology. However, this convergence is almost exclusively attributable to change within economics. [...] because the most important findings in neuroeconomics have posed more of a challenge to the standard economic perspective than to dominant perspectives within psychology. [...] much of the research in neuroscience and more recently neuroeconomics challenges the bedrock assumption within economics that decision-making is a unitary process—a simple matter of integrated and coherent utility maximization. (Loewenstein, Rick & Cohen 2008: 649)

2.3 RATIONALITY

"'Rationality' is a word with mostly favorable a priori connotations. No one readily thinks of his own actions as irrational, and few economists are comfortable with the idea of modeling irrational behavior. More specifically, however, what does—or should—'rationality' mean?" (B. Friedman 1979: 23). For someone not trained in economics, behaving rationally simply refers to sensible decisions, acting with purpose, reasoning, and weighing the pros and cons, at least when making an important decision. In economics, however, behaving rationally requires the collection of valid information on all alternatives (i.e., unbiased perception of the current situation and the decision's consequences),[8] the calculation of prospective costs and benefits, the ranking of all options, and finally choosing the best, the top-ranked option providing the highest utility, profit respectively. Since Bernoulli (1738, 1954) introduced psychology into decision theory, individuals' decisions are not simply

---

[8] Akerlof and Shiller (2015) describe how misperceptions are intentionally created in markets to "phish phools." Thaler and Sunstein (2008) show that "soft paternalism" can "nudge" into better decisions.

guided by expected monetary value (wealth) but rather by the perceived utility derived from wealth. What do firms maximize? Profits indeed rank high, but many firms have multidimensional goals (such as market share and identification with the firm), which increases the complexity of the choice process.

Utility is what people maximize, but what "utility" means remains unclear. Does it mean a higher income, bigger cars, more leisure, a happier life, a cleaner environment, more equality, or more of everything? "Rational choice" does not specify what is to be maximized; it can be anything as long as choices are consistent. It claims to be neutral because the individual should know best. "The analysis assumes that individuals maximise welfare as they conceive it, whether they be selfish, altruistic, loyal, spiteful, or masochistic" (Becker 1993a: 386). "Rational choice" focuses on the consistency of choices but allows for a high degree of freedom concerning individual tastes and preferences. "De gustibus on est dispudantum" (Stigler & Becker 1977) or "free to choose" (Friedman & Friedman 1990) without a value judgment; the individual can choose anything as long as the choices are consistent, they are regarded as rational (see Chapter 3). This led Sen (1977) to title a paper "Rational Fools" and allowed Becker (1965, 1993b) to apply "rational choice"— individual utility maximization—to all areas of life, from family to drug addiction and others more, claiming that "It is a method of analysis, not an assumption about particular motivation" (Becker 1993a: 385).

"Since Savage simultaneously axiomized utility and subjective probability we know what rational economic behavior is. Rational economic behavior is the maximization of subjectively expected utility" (Selten 1990). Utility maximization is defined from the end: If individuals are assumed to know their own preferences best and maximize, their observed choices should provide the highest expected utility among the myriad of ranked options.[9] Alternatives ordered by preference are assigned numbers, and the alternative with the highest number is chosen, "… we could christen this measure 'utility' and then assert that choices are made to maximize utility. It is an easy step to the statement that 'you are maximizing your utility,' which says no more than that your

---

[9]   Since utility is derived from observed choices but not measured directly, it is also labeled *indirect utility*. It is "expected" because when choosing utility is not experienced yet. Expected and experienced utility may deviate (see Chapters 4 and 5).

choice is predictable according to the size of some assigned numbers" (Alchian 1953: 31). "Some assigned numbers" is certainly less specific than Bernoulli's logarithm of wealth, but being unspecific may protect against falsification. "Utility is a metaphysical concept of impregnable circularity; utility is the quality in commodities that makes individuals want to buy them, and the fact that individuals want to buy commodities shows that they have utility" (Robinson 1962: 48). Are observed choices maximizing expected utility? One equation with two unknown variables:

$$Ui(max) = Ui(preference)$$

Ui(max): unobserved, maximum asserted

Ui(preference): unobserved

Where: $Ui(max)$ = individual's maximum utility for alternative i, $Ui(Preference)$ = individual's expected utility derived from the preferred alternative.

Simon (1986) observed that it has never been shown that observed choices reveal the individual optimum (i.e., the highest-ranked alternative). It is simply asserted; it rests on the rationality assumption. "[If] one can observe utility functions directly, then we can check whether the neo-classical marginalist assumption holds" (van Praag & Ferrer-i-Carbonell 2008: 335). As long as utility is not observed directly but simply deduced under the rationality axioms from observed choices, the theory is immune to falsification. If the null hypothesis (the validity of maximization) is unsubstantiated, it is simply assumed to be the outcome of "rational choice." "This is somewhat like arm wrestling a rag doll; it doesn't prove anything—unless the rag doll wins" (Conlisk 1996: 684–685).

Wansbeek and Kapteyn (1983: 249) wrote:

Utility is to economists what the Lord is to theologians. Economists talk about utility all the time, but do not seem to have hope of ever observing it this side of heaven. In micro-economic theory, almost every model is built on utility functions of some kind. In empirical work little attempt is made to measure this all-pervasive concept.

"Rational choice" is logically deduced from the premises (maximization); it is a normative concept. As Ramsey (1926: 193) explains: "Logic, we may agree, is concerned not with what men actually believe, but what they ought to believe, or what it would be reasonable to believe." In short, "rational choice" is normative. It prescribes how individuals should decide to follow the premises. Allais (1953) argued that the internal consistency of the axioms and deduced behavior could be analyzed or "rationality can be defined experimentally by observing the actions of people who can be regarded as acting in a rational manner" (504). This is the approach of Behavioral Economics where numerous experiments have been performed to investigate decision-making and to test the validity of the neoclassical axioms, suggesting that, for example, the assumption of stable preferences does not hold because experience, habit formation, and tastes may change preferences. Therefore, Keynes contended that the problem is the axioms and not the superstructure. The neoclassical axioms limit the space of possibilities for analysis and oblige the analysts to follow the logic (a mathematical exercise, Ramsey 1926) and enforce internal coherence. Following the laws of logic, behavior deduced from a set of axioms may apply to the resulting artificial world, but *in the economy we live in*, deviations from the conditions of "rational choice" are dominant. "If rationality is to be defined as adherence to one of the system's axioms which leads to a Bernoulli type formulation, then obviously no discussion is possible. Such a definition, therefore, has no interest per se" (Allais 1953: 504).

It is often claimed that the ranking of alternatives is relative (i.e., the magnitude of differences in the utilities remains unmeasured), which contradicts the concept of expected utility which is the product of pure utility according to the preferences multiplied by their probability. Bernoulli uses the logarithm of wealth as utility—a cardinal measure— and Marshall (1890) argued that the price equals the marginal utility, which seems to provide a (although indirect) measure to rank the various options.

Whereas utility maximization is simply assumed, based on the neo-classical axioms but remains unmeasured, happiness studies aim to measure well-being directly, asking how people are satisfied with their life in general or with specific circumstances (see, e.g., Layard 2005, van Praag & Ferrer-i-Carbonell 2008, Frey & Stutzer 2002, Clark, Frijters & Shields 2008). Based on questionnaires, respondents usually classify their well-being on a scale from 1 to 10, which is interpreted as a cardinal measure (van Praag & Ferrer-i-Carbonell 2008). Measurement issues aside, the most significant difference is directly measured "life-satisfaction" to the assumed (indirect) utility maximization deduced from the rationality axioms. In addition, the direct measurement is historical, asking about experienced rather than expected satisfaction. In contrast, utility is future-oriented and expected, as Clark et al. (2008) argue. Behavioral Economics distinguishes expected from experienced utility, and one could ask individuals about experienced utility on a 10-point scale. The different methodological approaches in logical science emphasize the internal consistency of behavior deduced from the axioms versus real science. In Behavioral Economics, history influences utility perception, as exemplified by reference points such as "comparison to oneself" (Clark et al. 2008).

Why did an axiomatic concept with extremely stringent assumptions become the yardstick for economic decision theory, the *sine qua non* of good economic theory (Akerlof & Yellen 1987: 137)? "We make an about face and rely on indirect statistical inference to derive the unknown structural relationships from the observed magnitudes of prices, outputs and other variables that, in our role as theoreticians, we treated as unknowns" (Leontief 1971: 4).

2.4   EQUILIBRIUM: BALANCE OR OPTIMUM?

Diverging notions of equilibrium are at the root of the dispute between Keynes' theory and the neoclassical General Equilibrium model. In Keynes' theory, as in physics, equilibrium is a state of rest in which individual forces compensate each other, a balanced situation without any notion of the quality of the equilibrium and no automatic mechanism guiding the economy out of suboptimal positions. In contrast, the neoclassical equilibrium concept refers to the welfare optimum of the economy given the economy's resources and institutional frame.[10] The differences between the two concepts are in the microeconomic reasoning, in the intention and ability of individuals and firms to maximize, and in the effectiveness of the price mechanism to compensate for deviations in demand and supply. If all actions and reactions occur instantaneously, the economy will always be at its optimum. Already time-lags will disturb the harmony, and the economy will be at least shortly out of equilibrium, out of welfare optimum. "In contrast to most physical sciences, we study a system that is not only exceedingly complex but is also in a state of constant flux" (Leontief 1971: 3).

What leads the economy to achieve the welfare optimum in the neoclassical model? Each individual is assumed to achieve their optimum

---

[10]   Tobin (1972: 4) suggests viewing Keynes' equilibrium as "persistent disequilibrium." This label, however, seems to imply that the welfare optimum of the neoclassical model is the true "equilibrium," although Keynes emphasized that the neoclassical equilibrium is comprised in his theory. His main point was that the economy might be trapped in underemployment equilibrium because the assumed endogenous mechanism to push the economy to the optimum is missing.

in this model, but the "invisible hand" is claimed to coordinate the selfish individual actions of *homo oeconomicus* to the societal optimum. The insatiable, restless *homo oeconomicus* who knows their stable and well-ordered preferences determined in isolation and searches continuously for improvements of the utility-maximizing combination depending on relative prices and assigned probabilities (see Chapter 4.1). Independent preferences formed without interactions with other individuals other than market exchange allow the sum of individual utility to be declared the societal optimum. However, the *first fundamental theorem* of welfare economics states that a competitive market economy coordinates individual activity to the most efficient allocation of resources to a point at which no further improvements are possible (see Stiglitz 1986). Competitive markets are thought to achieve the maximum or optimum output through individual maximization steered by the *invisible hand*. Every economic agent uses all possibilities to improve their situation following the marginal principle where marginal benefits and efforts (costs) balance. The restless *homo oeconomicus* searches for improvements until no person can improve their utility without harming someone else's: the Pareto equilibrium achieved through voluntary exchange.[11] This difference in the equilibrium concepts, balance versus optimum, is ingrained in the fundamental assumptions of humans' motivations and abilities and the functioning of markets.

"The simplest case of balance or equilibrium between desire and effort is found when a person satisfies one of his wants by his own direct work" (Marshall 1890: 331). Marshall uses berry-picking to illustrate that the individual's equilibrium is achieved when the marginal utility of the last berry picked equals the effort to pick it. Picking berries is an effort, devoid of direct utility; no fun to pick berries. When this point is achieved depends on individual preferences, whether or not someone likes berries and has access to them.[12] The easier berries are to pick, the more will be

---

[11]   This is usually illustrated with the Edgeworth Box. Stiglitz (1986) emphasizes that the Pareto criterium ignores the initial distribution of resources and therefore an infinite amount of Pareto optima depending on the distribution of resources exists. An utility increase of the wealthiest is set similar to that of the least wealthiest (which is in conflict with the declining marginal utility of wealth).

[12]   This is the basis for the neoclassical production function: easily accessible berries are picked first with little effort (high marginal productivity), then those which require a higher effort etc. The neoclassical production function describes

picked with given preferences. Similarly, for observed voluntary transactions, the individual is thought to be in "equilibrium" in the exchange of goods, meaning that their marginal utility of good A equals that of the alternative good B. However, observations suggest that the price for purchasing A is lower than the price for giving up A. This has been observed for bottles of wine, tickets to concerts and sporting events, and even for coffee mugs (see Kahneman 2011).

"Classical General Equilibrium Theory assumes that every agent knows all prices and that every agent has all the information that is needed about every good" (Hahn 1980: 134). It is a significant intellectual achievement that Arrow and Debreu (1954) could demonstrate that a set of prices under very specific conditions could make the decentralized decisions of utility-maximizing households and profit-maximizing firms compatible such that the demand and supply for any good are equal. Especially Arrow (e.g., 1986) reminded economists that solving a system of well-defined equations is not proof that the *economy we live in* functions according to these equations. For example, the model does not account for imperfect competition (oligopolies, coalitions, collusion, increasing returns), non-convex preferences, uncertainty and expectations, information asymmetries, transaction costs,[13] and the fact that not all goods are traded in markets at any time, that future markets for most goods do not exist, exchange is contracted in monetary terms instead of relative prices (real values, the exchange ratio of goods). Money is simply regarded as a veil covering the exchange proportions, the ratio of quantities. Trade may take place at non-market-clearing prices. It is an exchange system based on relative price—ratios of goods—rather than a monetary economy. "Why should the average level of prices be affected significantly by changes in the prices of some things relative to others?" (Friedman 1975: 73). Money prices and monetary policy can only affect individuals and the economy by error. Money is a veil hiding the real proportions.

---

the extraction of natural resources and agriculture well but hardly the production of manufactures which usually require high initial development costs whereas the production costs are low (declining marginal costs). An extreme case is standard software where the development is extremely costly but additional units are produced at minimal costs. In textbooks production functions with declining marginal costs are used to illustrate monopolies but declared to be exceptions.

13 Ignoring transaction costs is ignoring time (Coase 1937).

In addition, work is a choice variable in the neoclassical model, where utility is maximized in a combination of leisure and work (income). Workers supply their labor until the marginal value of work (income) equals the marginal utility of leisure.[14] If the individual's optimum is disturbed, they will immediately adjust their consumption and working pattern accordingly; therefore, any disturbance would be exogenous and short-lived. When no more improvements are possible, and all options for voluntary trade have been exhausted, the equilibrium is Pareto optimal. This exposition has enormous consequences for economic policy: If the economy is at or near optimum already, there is, of course, no need for any stimulating macroeconomic policy. The only option to improve the economy's welfare (utility) is to change the incentive structure to adjust the institutional framework, which allows for a higher optimum (see discussion in Chapter 7). This idea, implemented in the knowledge base of the neoclassical model, is most pronounced in the neoclassical counterrevolution framed as the "natural rate of unemployment" and is the base for the neoliberal policy proposals of President Reagan of the United States and Prime Minister Thatcher of the United Kingdom.

Although the optimal equilibrium is not empirically established but simply deduced from numerous idealistic assumptions, it is often used as a starting point for analyses. Of course, if the analysis assumes the economy to be at the optimum (full employment), macroeconomic stimulation could only harm; it would push the economy away from that optimum, leading to higher prices but not to expanded production. This is precisely what Keynes concluded for an economy at the optimum, at full employment (Keynes 1936). However, the neoclassical model limits itself to situations where the full employment assumption actually holds. But the welfare optimum—full employment—is a unique situation, resting on the assumed automatic market mechanism to full employment. Without the "invisible hand" directing markets to the optimum, Keynes argued that economies might well get stuck in suboptimal situations, less than full employment. He challenged all the sacred ingredients of neoclassical economics: The "invisible hand" does not work; markets, first of all, the labor market, do not necessarily clear by price variations.[15] Say's law does not hold, supply may not create its demand, unexploited opportunities may exist, and the economy may get stuck in a suboptimal

---

[14]   The neoclassical labor supply model (see Chapter 7).
[15]   See also Kalmbach (1985).

equilibrium where external expansionary impulses (fiscal or monetary) can move the economy closer to the optimum. The neoclassical analysis usually starts in equilibrium based on real values, but neoclassical economics says nothing about "disequilibrium" (see Rothschild 1981). Again, the axioms of the neoclassical model set the standard; disequilibrium usually describes a deviation from the optimum of full employment. The deduced unique equilibrium is the model's strength and, at the same time, its weakness because it depends on so many unrealistic assumptions.

2.5   THE LEVEL OF ANALYSIS: MICRO OR MACRO?

"Micro" refers to the behavior and decisions of individual people and firms; "macro" refers to aggregates like investment and consumption. "Macro" consists of a myriad of micro-units thought to be coordinated by the "invisible hand." Still, economic behavior at the macro level is not identical with the sum of individual economic activities because of competition, interactions, heterogeneity of the micro-units' myriad of micro decisions. How can all of these micro-decisions be aggregated to the macro level? One possibility is "bottom-up": modeling the economic behavior of individuals and firms and aggregating them to the entire economy. Such a micro-simulation is the most ambiguous and complicated approach. Even under the strictest rules of behavior, complex dynamics may occur if heterogeneous agents are considered (see Albin 1998). Another bottom-up method would be to average the characteristics and reactions of individuals and take them as representing the economic behavior of the aggregate. This method ignores the interdependencies and interactions. A third method would be to construct a representative agent simulating the behavior of the aggregate. But this detour is similar to using the aggregate (e.g., overall consumption), and one may better utilize the aggregate directly (Kirman 1992).

In his influential critique on predictions of economic policy effects based on historic coefficients, Lucas (1972) argued that individual reactions to policy depend on (rational) expectations, not on past behavior (Chapter 5 and 7). Keynes would certainly not disagree with the importance of expectations for individual decisions of consumers, workers, entrepreneurs, investors, and speculators, but he indeed denies the applicability of rational expectations. Lucas claimed that individuals react according to the neoclassical axioms and that science requires the aggregate to be traced back to the individual. This was not the birth[16] but indeed the application of the "representative agent."

Microfoundations describe the behavior of individuals and firms, but the term is often used to claim neoclassical axioms as the basis for economic analysis. Anything else is flawed; scientific rigor requires the analysis based on maximization and equilibrium; neoclassical microfoundations (Lucas & Sargent 1978). For example, overall consumer demand in the economy is thought to behave similarly to individual consumption; the macro is treated like the micro. But how do the individuals' and firms' decisions result in coordinated, well-behaving macro relations? The simplest assumption is that all individuals and firms are identical, follow the same preferences, react similarly to price and income variations, and are in individual equilibrium at their maximum utility or profits. One may also think of a representative agent who behaves as the aggregate. However, having a single unit to represent the aggregate requires very restrictive conditions.[17] Jackson and Yariv (2020) explain that individual indirect utility functions must have linear and identical Engels curves[18] that depend only on income. Summarizing their findings: "They illustrate an impossibility result for wide classes of utility functions, including practically all those studied in the literature" (Jackson & Yariv 2020: 17).

If the micro-units are assumed to act independently from each other, if they are supposed to maximize their own utility with stable preferences, the aggregate may be considered identical to the sum of individual actions, that is, assuming that the macroeconomy is simply the sum of independent microeconomic decisions. A situation in which outcomes can be computed by the multiplication of individual actions. Macro is merely a multiple of micro. Even if not all individuals behave identically, the argument goes, deviations in both directions and their average—the representative agent—will fit the deduced behavior. The neoclassical model limits interactions between individual units to market exchange. The choices and attitudes of other individuals do not affect their pref-

---

[16]   Jackson and Yariv (2020) mention that Edgeworth referred to a "representative particular" and Marshall to a "representative firm."

[17]   The idea of the aggregate representative demand (D) leads to the same reactions to prices as the individual reactions summed up: (Jackson & Yariv 2020: 1); see also Kirman (1992).

[18]   Engels curves describe the structure of expenditures as a function of income.

erences; they simply adjust to changing relative prices. Rising demand for some products may raise their relative prices (the exchange ratios of goods) and may lead to adjustments along the preference functions to achieve the new utility optimum within budget constraints. But these adjustments are only due to changes in prices. The preferences, the utility functions remain unchanged. Rising demand for some products does not affect the desire to own these products; there are no fashions, no trends, no hype, no herd behavior. Such a system is hypothetical not descriptive to *the world we live in.*

Suppose every individual maximizes utility along with independent and stable preference functions in a stable environment. In that case, the economy's utility maximum may be defined as the sum of individual utility:[19] the optimum. The same argument is made for firms and profits. Firms, the argument goes, are forced to apply optimal— profit-maximizing—techniques to survive in competitive markets; survival of the fittest. Producing at higher costs with less efficient technology will lead to the extinction of the firm because, in perfect markets, higher costs and prices will shift demand to competitors. Under some conditions, markets may constantly force firms to search for optimal production techniques. This argument, however, can hardly apply to individuals; they will not be extinguished if they do not maximize utility continuously; only *homo oeconomicus* survives? The concept of perfect competition ignores market power and assumes that individual rationality results in social rationality.

Summarized in *Micromotives and Macrobehavior,* Schelling (1978) impressively showed that micro "rationality" might not produce macro "rationality." One example is the requirement that hockey players wear helmets. In the past, hockey was played without helmets, and although the players understood the associated risk well, they avoided the marginal disadvantage of wearing helmets. Schelling's solution was to make helmets compulsory. The slight marginal disadvantage of wearing a helmet will affect all players, the relative position remains unchanged, and their health and safety improved. In another example, Schelling shows that although every citizen prefers a somewhat integrated neighborhood, individual decisions unintentionally produce a totally segre-

---

[19]   Adding up utility requires cardinal measurement, the interpersonal comparability of utility, which is usually thought to be impossible.

gated city. Individual decision-making leads to a macro situation that violates everybody's preferences, an ecological fallacy.

Ignoring interactions among individuals is undoubtedly an oversimplification but simply mirroring the request for the microfoundations of macroeconomics by a request for macro-foundations of microeconomics also seems unsatisfactory. "But this position is rarely developed and often leaves unexplained how the macroeconomic aggregates relate to individual decisions" (Chick 2016: 99). Basing the analysis on the behavior of aggregates, the macro also needs to make assumptions about the behavior of micro-units (i.e., these to remain unchanged, or balance) and that interactions do not change. The causation does not run in one direction from micro to macro or vice versa; one process affects another. Whereas in the neoclassical model, supply determines demand, Keynes' fundamental innovation was limited demand. Furthermore, in the *General Theory,* it is expected future demand, and here *time* and *uncertainty* are important (effective demand). It may be analytically necessary to focus on one side, but when doing so, the scholar must remember that a partial model cannot always be applied one-to-one to *the world we live in.*[20] To be sure, the options for individual choice depend on macroeconomic conditions. Still, the macroeconomic outcomes also depend on individual decisions, as exemplified by Keynes' effective demand: tomorrow's income and production depend on today's decisions on investment.

Hiring and job search also exemplify the interactions of micro and macro. From the micro perspective, job search of the employed (on-the-job search) crowds out the unemployed (Burgess 1993), which may well apply for specific jobs but is misleading when generalized. Under unchanged economic conditions, a vacancy filled by an employed job seeker will lead to a vacancy at his former establishment, which may be filled by an unemployed job seeker (Gorter & Schettkat 2009). Crowding out between employed and unemployed job seekers depends on the stage of the macroeconomy on the level of employment.

Some Keynesians emphasize that it does not need individual behavior deviating from "homo economicus" (i.e., from the axioms of neoclassical economics) to establish Keynes' underemployment equilibrium. Time lags (missing full information or the substitutes "the auctioneer") are suf-

---

[20]   If individuals' interactions are restricted to market exchanges, if the individual is isolated from society and everybody is the same, the aggregation problem is assumed away. See also Elsner (2012).

ficient to establish suboptimal equilibria. It does not need an alternative micro theory; the missing auctioneer is sufficient. "The only thing which Keynes 'removed' from the foundations of classical theory was the deux ex machina—the auctioneer who is assumed to furnish, without charge, all the information needed to obtain the perfect coordination of the activities of all traders in the present and through the future" (Leijonhufvud 1967: 410). True, achieving the optimal equilibrium in the neoclassical model depends on many critical assumptions, of which just one needs to be withdrawn to get diverging results. But what is the point? Just to show that the optimal equilibrium of the artificial Walrasian system critically depends on the assumptions? Was Keynes' ambition only to show that the neoclassical results depend on critical assumptions? Keynes made clear that economic theory needs to relate to *the world we live in* and that useful economic theory cannot totally abstract from reality.

2.6 UNCERTAINTY AND PROBABILITY

Uncertainty is often used synonymously for all situations that are not certain but depend on probabilities (see Table 2.1). Knight (1921) and Keynes (1921, for economic decisions, especially 1936, 1937) distinguished uncertainty from risk, which has severe consequences for economic theory. "Rational choice" depends on the ability to calculate expected values or utility, which requires known probabilities; it is not applicable under uncertainty. The wording and specific meaning of uncertainty are confusing, ranging from true, objective, unmeasurable uncertainty, ambiguity,[21] slightly uncertain, over risk, to certainty.[22] In this book, uncertainty is used for true uncertainty, and risk is used for events where probabilities are known.

---

[21] Ambiguity is often used synonymous to uncertainty in Keynes' sense as in Ellsberg (1961). In many papers uncertainty is used to describe all situations which are not certain. Einhorn and Hogarth (1986) distinguish exact from ambiguous uncertainty where exact uncertainty describes risk and explains that the outcome of flipping coins is uncertain but not ambiguous since the probabilities are well specified (S229).

[22] Some authors draw distinctions among true, immeasurable or fundamental uncertainty, where probabilities cannot be known, while uncertainty is where probabilities can be known in principle, but are unknown for the decider (Dow 2012). Knight (1921) used "measurable uncertainty" to describe risk and "unmeasurable uncertainty" to describe true uncertainty.

Table 2.1   Degrees of uncertainty

True uncertainty	Subjective uncertainty	Risk	Certainty
Events do not follow a probability distribution	Events follow a probability distribution, but it is unknown to the individual	Events follow a probability distribution known to the individual	The "sure thing"

The distinction between risk and uncertainty may be illustrated with the roulette game: The next number is unknown when playing roulette, but every number has a 1 in 37 probability of appearing. This, however, is the relative frequency after an infinite number of repetitions when the "law of large numbers" applies. The next number may be anything between 0 and 36.[23] The expected value of betting on a specific number is the payoff multiplied by the probability minus the inset ($36X * 1/37 - X$, where X is the inset). Still, the individual bet wins ($36*X - X$) or loses ($-X$). Betting is always risky. Still, the chances can be calculated; expected values can be calculated, which has been commonplace in economics since Bernoulli's (1738, 1954) work.[24] In uncertain situations, "we simply do not know" (Keynes 1937: 214) and cannot know the long-run price or interest trends. Keynes argued that economic decisions, like most real-life decisions, are made under uncertainty and doubted the usefulness of normative rationality:

> Business men play a mixed game of skill and chance, the average results of which to the players are not known by those who take a hand. If human nature felt no temptation to take a chance, no satisfaction (profit apart) in constructing a factory, a railway, a mine, or a farm, there might not be much investment merely as a result of cold calculation. (Keynes 1936: 150)

Like Schumpeter's (1911) entrepreneurial spirit, Keynes emphasizes the joy of doing rather than as a simple burden.

---

[23]   Aside from shifting chances in their favor (the zero in roulette) casinos make sure that the law of large numbers cannot work for the gambler by limiting the bets to a maximum (for other useful hints: Taleb 2007). Payoffs to insets are biased in favor for casinos although varying internationally.

[24]   It is risky to bet, but gamblers may feel their chance to win to be higher than 1 in 37, probably because their favorite number was not drawn for so long.

Certainly, for investment, the pros and cons will be evaluated, affecting the confidence of the decision-maker but not the probability; the final decision depends on emotions or animal spirits, as supported by recent findings in the neurological sciences. Many economists, even Keynesians, are uncomfortable with animal spirits and prefer to keep the concept of rational choice in their analysis. But how do individuals maximize and choose rationally if the probability distribution is unknown? Knowing the probability distribution does not reveal anything about individual trials; it only applies to "big numbers," which is "Bernoulli's error" (see the distinction between ensemble average and time average, Chapters 3 and 5).

> Yet the feeling persisted that, even in these situations, people tend to *behave* "as though" they assigned numerical probabilities, or "degrees of belief," to the events impinging on their actions. However, it is hard either to confirm or to deny such a proposition in the absence of precisely defined procedures for *measuring* these alleged "degrees of belief." (Ellsberg 1961: 643, italics in original)[25]

Ellsberg refers to the concept of subjective probability (Friedman & Savage 1948, 1952), which claims to transform uncertainty into risk, and this way allows to apply rational decision theory. Subjective probability, which is a feeling or a guess, has been labeled by Ramsey (1926) as "human logic" and was later applied to economics by Von Neumann and Morgenstern (1944) and Friedman and Savage (1948, 1952). Subjective probability starts from the end: Assuming that "rational man" chooses the option which provides maximum utility (profits, respectively) composed of the assigned preferences and their probability. Assuming the individual chooses rationally, she must have subjective probabilities in her calculations. Even under uncertainty, or unknown true probabilities, the choice is subjectively "rational." However, subjective expected utility (SEU) makes observed choices formally consistent with the rationality axioms by adding another unobserved variable to the equation in section 2.3 (see Chapter 4).

Do decisions made under conditions of probability and uncertainty deviate? Ellsberg (1961) designed an experiment to prove Savage's axiom

---

[25]   Ellsberg (1961) used "ambiguity" similar to Keynes' uncertainty or what Keynes called "non-comparable probability" in the *Treatise on Probability* (1921).

similar to Keynes' thought experiment in his *Treatise on Probability*, finding that subjects violate "rational choice," meaning they assign inconsistent probabilities when confronted with uncertain situations where they allegedly establish subjective probabilities. From an individual's perspective, probabilities may be unknown because (1) they are ignorant; (2) they do not make the effort to discover the probabilities although they could be detected in principle; (3) it is impossible to assign meaningful probabilities to specific events (genuine uncertainty), and (4) many kinds of individual decisions are unique. Shackle (1958: 5–6) summarized the conditions:

> It follows that in forming expectations, actuarial general principles and particular facts will only help us when the following conditions are satisfied: (1) We are sure that the system, whose future behaviour we wish to know, will remain a given system and not undergo changes during the interval of future time in question. (2) We are interested only in the total result of a "large number" of trials, all of which count equally or virtually so in building up this total. (3) We feel sure that we shall, in fact, have the opportunity to carry out a sufficient number of trials, and not, for example, find that our plans depended, in fact, on the successful issue of a few early trials whose failure has deprived us of the means of continuing. In many of the most important affairs of life these conditions are not fulfilled.

Applying probability distributions requires the economy to remain stable and not undergo substantial changes in the future. The assumption of "rational expectations" is a form of stochastic perfect foresight (Arrow 1986). Still, the economy's path is not exogenously determined but open, affected by decisions of economic agents. To Keynes, this entailed "effective demand": expectations about the future affect today's investment, employment, and future production potential, a dynamic approach. But Keynes did not develop a dynamic methodology as Harrod (1937) immediately criticized in his remarks on the *General Theory*. Economic decisions are always future-oriented, and even if events follow a probability distribution, it is unknown and cannot be established by observing repeated events. Furthermore, the payoffs (or the utility) are often undefined in *the economy we live in*. How can "rational choices," calculated outcomes (profit, values, utility) be made?

In his *General Theory*, Keynes referred to uncertainty, especially relevant for investment decisions that require a long time horizon where businessmen are feeling or pretending to know probabilities which led to specific investment decisions. But it only seems to be based on calculations; probabilities are unknown and cannot be known under uncertainty.[26] It seems that Keynes became more aware of the relevance of uncertainty for economic decisions while writing the *General Theory*. In his *Treatise on Probability*, based on his 1904 thesis but published in 1921 (Skidelsky 2003),[27] Keynes analyzes fundamental issues of knowledge (epistemology) and uses "uncertainty"[28] with reference to induction:

> In other words, Pure Induction can be usefully employed to strengthen an argument, after a certain number of instances have been examined, we have, from some other source, a finite probability in favour of the generalisation as to its conclusion been satisfied by the next hitherto unexamined instance which satisfies its premises. (Keynes 1921: 238)

Certainly, Keynes was most emphatic on uncertainty concerning economic decisions in his 1937 article when he wrote:

> By "uncertain" knowledge, let me explain, I do not mean merely to distinguish what is known for certain from what is only "probable" [...] About these matters there is no scientific basis on which to form any calculable probability whatever. We simply do not know. Nevertheless, the necessity for action and for decision compels us as practical men to do our best to overlook this awkward fact and to behave exactly as we should if we had behind us a good Benthamite calculation of a series of prospective advantages and disadvantages, each multiplied by its appropriate probability, waiting to be summed. (213–214).[29]

Some commentators such as Pasinetti (2007) argue that Keynes' thoughts on the consequences of uncertainty for economic decisions were stimulated by discussions with his colleagues Kahn and Robinson, and it seems

---

[26] The title of Knight's book, *Risk, Uncertainty, and Profit* (1921) indicates that Knight was concerned with business decisions.

[27] The title of Skidelsky's biography *John Maynard Keynes 1983–1946, Economist, Philosopher, Statesman* indicates Keynes' brought interest and knowledge.

[28] Keynes (1921) uses uncertainty to describe the understanding of probability (page 51), to its relevance for inductions (86, 238, 266–267). with reference to "mathematical expectations (313), and distinguishes uncertainty from risk ("[...], in spite of the uncertainty of each particular case" 337).

[29] Similarly Nelson and Winter (1982: 94) argue: "Orthodoxy treats the skillful behavior of the businessman as maximizing choice, and "choice" carries connotations of "deliberation." We on the other hand, emphasize the automaticity of skillful behavior and the suppression of choice that this involves."

that Keynes' view of human nature changed from the traditional view in economics to one which includes emotions and conventional wisdom (Barnett 2017). The *General Theory* received enormous attention right from its publication, but since Keynes departed substantially from neo-classical assumptions, it was hard even for the sympathetic economist to understand. Therefore, Hicks' (1937) interpretation of the *General Theory*—first presented at a conference in Oxford discussing the *General Theory* (Keynes, Kahn, and Robinson were absent)—culminating in the IS-LM diagram which became widely accepted and is often equated with Keynesian economics.[30] The liquidity trap simply became the flat Keynesian part of the LM curve and eliminated the uncertainty in liquidity decisions.

Subjective probability may fit what Keynes referred to as probability as a degree of belief about future events, but he emphasized believing a probability is not a true probability. The subjective probability of the gambler putting all his money on the 13 because it has not appeared for such a long time is certainly unrelated to the probability of the next draw being a 13. He certainly intends to increase his wealth but when leaving the casino, his expression may show that he seriously misunderstood the concept of probability.

2.7   MARKETS AND TIME: HOW DO MARKETS CLEAR?

Markets coordinate the innumerous individual economic actions to an ordered outcome; they find the price vector at which the maximum number of sellers and buyers are served, and the economy achieves its welfare optimum. Although everyone maximizes their individual utility and profit, the myriad of selfish actions will be directed to the optimal outcome by price variations. Prices will lead markets to equilibrium, but how a decentralized economy finds the market-clearing price remains a black box, as Smith's metaphor of the "invisible hand" illustrates. Critiques claim "[…] the reason that the invisible hand often seemed to be invisible was, that it wasn't there" (Stiglitz 2012). "An intriguing paradox was involved in stating that the *general* interest and welfare

---

[30]   See also Hansen's (1953) textbook *A Guide to Keynes.* In the US literature the IS-LM diagram is occasionally referred to as the Hicks-Hansen diagram.

would be promoted by the self-interested activities of numerous decentralized operators" (Hirschman 1992: 44, emphasis in original).

Equilibrium in individual markets is at the crossing of the demand function sloping downwards with marginal utility and the supply function sloping upwards with marginal costs. Deviation from this equilibrium will be adjusted by price variations, just as Marshall (1890) explained in his *Principles of Economics*. Every economics student learns this message in the very first lectures, and contemporary textbooks still use Marshall's market diagram (Figure 2.1) to illustrate the functioning of a (partial) market. The market is cleared at price P* and quantity Q*; sellers do not want to sell more, and buyers do not demand more at the equilibrium price (P*). Marshall argued that left of the equilibrium quantity (Q* in Figure 2.1), the demand function (D) lies above the supply function (S), and buyers have an incentive to purchase and this way, bidding up the price allowing for higher supply covering the rising marginal costs with higher quantities produced. Right of the equilibrium supply exceeds demand and, so the argument goes, prices will move towards the market-clearing price (P*). Markets are clearing if not disturbed by government, regulation, etc.

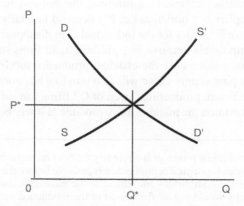

Source: Inspired by Marshall (1890), Figure 19, or any microeconomic textbook.

Figure 2.1   Marshall's market diagram

In Marshall's market diagram suppliers are ranked according to their reservation prices (the minimum prices). Demand is ranked in the reverse direction. To establish the ranking, auxiliary institutions such as the auctioneer are required.

Marshall's market diagram, however, presents theoretical and hypothetical relations in timeless price–quantity space. One may ask how the market, how supply and demand actually come into existence. In the conventional market diagram, producers are ranked according to their marginal costs (which equal the price), but who knows these costs? Do firms with low and high costs produce and then wait to see whether they can sell their products (assumed to be homogeneous in a market), or does the supply function develop over time, and does the process start with the low-cost producers? If the market achieved equilibrium at P* and Q*, producers right of Q*—who produce at high costs—should disappear because they cannot sell. Similarly, if competition selects the fittest, why is not every firm producing with the low-cost technology, at least in the long run? Why are not all firms producing with the lowest cost technology like those firms on the very left of the quantity axis? The narrative is that competition selects the fittest, those firms that use the most efficient production technique. Are the responses symmetric? Does a price rise have the inverse effect of decline? Keynes argued that quantities rather than prices adjust.

When the market achieves equilibrium, the demand function for the individual supplier is a horizontal at P*; demand is totally price elastic. For prices above P*, order for the individual firm disappears, and pricing below P* is impossible because, in equilibrium, all firms should produce at the same costs since only the efficient producers survive. Therefore, the upward-sloping supply curve will also turn to a horizontal function at P*, the most efficient production.[31] Left of Q* firms can survive, but why do they not champion the market? They produce at lower costs, and com-

---

[31]   The most efficient producer is obviously the firm far to the left on the quantity scale. Although less efficient production is possible before the alleged market process reaches the equilibrium and enforces the most efficient production at lowest costs. Why would not all firms shift to the production technology of the far left firm?

Perfect competition requires small firms without any power to influence the market, that is diseconomies of scale. However, the upward sloping supply function may occur if firms produce with a neoclassical production (requiring diseconomies or constant economies of scale) and expand production which leads to rising marginal costs. In a (perfectly) competitive economy firms would produce with the most efficient technology (costs). Arguably more realistic is that firms produce with different technologies which would justify the upward sloping

petition should force other firms to imitate their production technology. Or why do not all firms shift to the most efficient technology? Since the supply function is assumed to represent marginal costs, suppliers right of the quantity Q* must leave the market because their marginal costs are above the price buyers are prepared to pay. The competitive pressure led only the efficient firms to survive, also turning the supply curve to a horizontal.

Marshall's market diagram is timeless; it does not indicate how the market came into existence or how it can ever get to a position deviating from the equilibrium if prices are assumed to react instantaneously. Usually, textbooks do not explain why markets could be out of equilibrium but simply state "for whatever reason" and then explain the adjustment to the equilibrium along with the functions. Actually, finding the equilibrium is not as logical as the narrative around Marshall's market diagram suggests, which assumes full information about the supply and demand functions. If these were common knowledge under the assumption of perfect information, the market-clearing price and quantity could be computed. The phrase "naturally ordered," meaning to rank suppliers from the lowest to highest price and consumers from highest to lowest price, leads to the required function, but who determines the ranking? The auctioneer who is absent in most markets?

How do markets evolve? Schumpeter (1911) argued that innovations initiate new markets and destroy existing markets, what he called creative destruction; that is, markets evolve. An innovative, new product is sold initially at a high price providing high monopoly profits. Still, some consumers are nevertheless attracted by the novelty and are prepared to pay the high price (T1 in Figure 2.2). The short-run supply function may be upward sloping (as illustrated in the circled market diagram of Figure 2.2), but over time, the initial monopoly and the related profits will melt down because imitations increase competition and process innovations reduce production costs, leading to declining prices. In other words, over time, the supply increases, and costs and prices fall, resulting in a long-run downward sloping supply curve (S long run in Figure 2.2) as the news about the usefulness of the new product spread in a contagion-like process demand increases with the falling prices. Therefore, also the long-run supply function in a Schumpeter market

---

supply function. Then, however, the idea of the selection of the fittest cannot be kept.

is downward sloping, showing a very different pattern from the static market in Marshall's diagram.

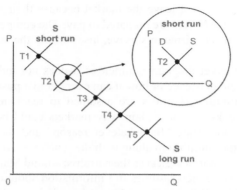

Note: In the short run supply increases with price and demand is downward sloping. Process innovations will reduce the production costs, allowing for higher quantities at lower prices. That is, the long run supply function is downward sloping indicated by the succession of short run situations T1 and following.
Source: Inspired by Schumpeter (1911).

Figure 2.2   Schumpeter's development of a market

However, even in Marshall's static market, participants have imperfect information. How can they know if prices paid deviate from the equilibrium price? How do firms set prices and know when to change prices to achieve maximum profit or adjust prices in response to adverse demand shocks? What happens if markets are not cleared, if the transactions are concluded at wrong prices—non-equilibrium prices? The simplest solution to problems arising from imperfect information is ignorance, simply assuming a perfect market with full information (known demand and supply functions), no adjustments costs, perfect competition. However, most economists would recognize that slow price reactions prevent markets from clearing instantaneously but would insist that prices move to the market-clearing price. Still, they nevertheless assume that the slow price reactions may delay but do not prevent the economy from achieving optimal equilibrium. That is, the short run is assumed not to affect the long run.

Under full information—in the "perfect market"—prices can react instantaneously, and therefore supply and demand never deviate from equilibrium. But this requires instantaneous price reactions; otherwise, the economy will at least shortly be out of equilibrium; one side of the market will be in excess, and transactions are made at non-equilibrium prices ("wrong prices"). Most economists would agree that the frictionless, perfect market may serve at best as a reference, but that the *economy we live in* suffers from imperfections that prevent the economy from achieving the optimal equilibrium instantaneously (in the short run, e.g., Blanchard & Wolfers 2000). Such reasoning is often ascribed to New Keynesian economics, which remains within the neoclassical equilibrium model but allows, for example, for price-adjustment costs (menu costs, Ball & Mankiw 1992; staggered contracts, Calvo 1983). Profit maximization may require delaying price adjustments in the short term because changing prices is costly (printing the menu). This, however, makes the optimization procedure even more complex.

Deviating from optimization are models that regard information on the demand and supply functions as incomplete, excluding optimal, profit-maximizing pricing. The unknown shape and location of the firm's demand function cause uncertainty over the profit consequences of price changes. Firms cannot calculate the profit-maximizing price and are reluctant to change prices (Greenwald & Stiglitz 1989, Hassink & Schettkat 2003). Although markets do not clear instantaneously, many economists nevertheless believe that the optimum is achieved in the long run, implying that short-term disequilibria do not affect the optimal equilibrium or the trend.[32] In other words, slow price reactions may delay but do not prevent achieving the optimal equilibrium, which would be instantaneously achieved in perfect markets, that is that an ergodic process is assumed. Does economic development follow an ergodic process, or may the short-term disturbance affect the equilibrium or the trend?

Marshall's demand and supply functions display buyers and sellers sorted by their reservation prices with prices determined by the marginal market participants. But in actual markets, neither sellers nor buyers are sorted by their reservation prices, and they suffer from insufficient information on unsatisfied demand and excess supply in a decentralized economy. In a decentralized market without full information in which contacts are random, and buyers with high reservation prices can make

---

[32] Leontief (1934) analyzed equilibrium conditions if production reacts with a delay on prices, known as cob-web models because whether the market converges to equilibrium or not depends on the elasticities of the demand and supply functions.

contact with sellers who demand low prices, bilateral contracts will be concluded at any price between the sellers' and the buyers' reservation prices. How do prices evolve in decentralized markets with partial information in which contacts of the market sides are random? Will the price converge to the market-clearing price, or will short-run deviations prevent it? Is the long-run result unaffected by short-run disequilibria? "Moving ahead in time, one 'short-run' follows the next 'short-run.' The long-run trend is a slowly changing component of a chain of short-period situations—it has no independent identity" (Kalecki 1971: 65). Technically (in physics, mathematics), processes that show the same outcome in the long run independently of the sequence of events are labeled ergodic and depend on negative feedback. That is, if prices rise, demand declines. Ergodic series are predictable and efficient; their long-run result is independent of the starting point or the sequence of events. In that case, ignoring market processes will not affect the long-run outcome (see Chapter 5.5). However, with positive feedback, the sequence of events matters and determines the outcomes; they are non-ergodic. For example, with declining marginal costs, firms may search for a large market share to achieve a cost advantage over competitors. Under economies of scale, and initially, a slight advantage will grow and may result in a "winner-takes-all market" (Arthur 1994b).

Actual markets do not resemble perfect markets, which are purely hypothetical. Several auxiliary assumptions intended to substitute for perfect information like an auctioneer who collects demand and supply information and announces the market-clearing price before transactions take place, or "tâtonnement" (a trial and error process initiated by an auctioneer), or re-contracting the correction of contracts concluded at wrong non-equilibrium prices and rational expectations where it is assumed that market participants know or learn the functions (Lucas 1986). These auxiliary institutions put forward to circumvent information imperfections scarcely exist in the economy we live in, where deviations from equilibrium prices and time lags between signals and response are common and where sequential decisions are the rule rather than the exception. Still, many economists insist on using equilibrium as a reference, if not for the short run, then for the long run.

Marshall's diagram gives an outsider view of an ordered market with hypothetical demand and supply functions. How does the market process evolve from a market participant's view, from the perspective of individual sellers and buyers in markets without an auctioneer, when contracts may be concluded at non-equilibrium ("wrong") prices? Chamberlin

(1948), who pioneered experiments in economics, constructed a market experiment in which he assigned each buyer a maximum purchasing price and each seller a minimum offering price. Sorting sellers and buyers by their reservation prices, the resulting demand and supply functions are sloped as in the conventional market diagram (Figure 2.1). The market-clearing price and quantity can be computed. However, in Chamberlin's market, information is imperfect; each participant buys or sells one product, market participants meet randomly and bargain with their contacts. They conclude a deal if they find a fit, that is if the seller's reservation price is below that of the buyer's. Prices are non-renegotiable. Those who completed contracts left the market, and prices of the last transactions were sometimes made public, sometimes not. It is crucial that bargaining and contracting were between individual buyers and sellers, different from an auction setting (as in V. Smith's experiment). Chamberlin did not confirm the convergence to market-clearing prices. On the contrary, prices fluctuated substantially before and even after the market hit equilibrium price. How can that happen?

In a conventional market diagram, buyers are sorted descending, and sellers ascending with their reservation prices—sometimes labeled natural—resulting in the usual downward sloping demand and upward sloping supply functions. If these functions are common knowledge (under full information) or if an auctioneer establishes the functions and computes the market-clearing price, buyers and sellers left of Q^* in Figure 2.1 are conceding deals, and those right of Q^* will remain unserved. And deals are only concluded at the market-clearing price. However, in Chamberlin's market, buyers and sellers make contact and negotiate the price. Chamberlin (1948: 97) summarizes: "In these forty-six experiments, the sales volume was higher than the equilibrium amount forty-two times and the same four times. It was never lower. The average price was higher than the equilibrium price seven times and lower thirty-nine times." Of course, experimental markets are not real markets, and students' behavior may differ from those of actual market participants. In computerized experiments simulating Chamberlin's market, Berczi (1979) found that although the price came closer to the theoretical market-clearing price, the traded volume was higher than the perfect market model predicted.

In a market where contracts are concluded randomly and successively, buyers with low reservation prices (those who are only prepared to pay a low price) may find a seller who asks for a low price. Contacts between sellers left from the market-clearing quantity (Q^*) and buyers right of

Q* are not excluded as in the full information "perfect" market case where transactions only occur at equilibrium prices and buyers with low reservation prices are excluded. It is also possible that buyers with high reservation prices contact sellers with high reservation prices. They may be served in a sequential market with individual contracting because transactions occur at non-equilibrium ("wrong") prices.

> The conclusion seems unavoidable that "price fluctuations render the volume of sales normally greater than the equilibrium amount which is indicated by the supply and demand curves," a proposition which must be of substantial importance in applying theory to the real economic world, since all actual markets, whether purely or monopolistically competitive, are more or less imperfect. (Chamberlin 1948: 98)

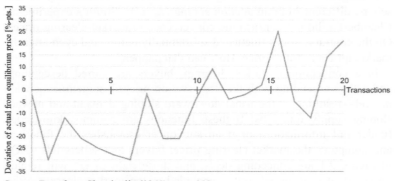

Source: Data from Chamberlin (1948), page 101.

Figure 2.3   Deviations of actual prices from the perfect competition equilibrium price (%pts.), Chamberlin's market experiment

Bilateral negotiations between sellers (who require a minimum price) and buyers (who determined their maximum prices) lead to contracts at "wrong" (non-equilibrium) prices. Buyers with reservation prices lower than the equilibrium price may get served if they make a contract with a supplier asking for a price below the equilibrium price. These buyers and sellers would have been excluded in a market coordinated by an auctioneer.

In his biographical note to the Nobel Prize Committee, V. Smith (2002b) explains that he participated as a student in one of Chamberlin's experiments at Harvard, which inspired him to work in experimental economics. "I decided to use the same value/cost setup but changed the institution. Secondly, I decided to repeat the experiment for several trading periods to allow the traders to obtain experience and to adapt over time, as in Marshall's conception of the dynamic competition" (V. Smith 2002b). The institution V. Smith used is a double auction in which buyers and sellers bid, and the organizing institution (usually the stock exchange) matches the bids which determines the price. He concludes from his market simulations and experiments that markets are even more efficient than the neoclassical model predicts because small groups (of four people) achieve market equilibrium in their transactions. However, his conclusion is based on an experiment where demand and supply information are matched. To demonstrate that such an institutional arrangement can achieve equilibrium prices and quantities as predicted with the market model of Figure 2.1 is, of course, no proof that actual markets function this way (except markets with double auctions). The fundamental question thus, is whether Chamberlin's experiment or V. Smith's experiment is more applicable for ordinary markets. Double auctions have the same problem as Walras auctioneer; the institution is missing in most markets.

The entrepreneur's reactions to an adverse demand shock depend on the signals' perception, interpretation, and timing. At first, the entrepreneur notices a decrease in demand for his product at unchanged prices; he will build up stocks. Only in the second step may he reduce production and/or lower the price. A rational decision requires estimates of the impact lower prices will have on the firm's turnover, which depends on the elasticity of demand. In a fully competitive market, the individual firm's demand function is totally elastic, and the price is not a variable for the firm to decide. But most firms have at least some discretion on prices; they face a downward-sloping demand function. Even in the extreme of a monopolist, finding the profit-maximizing price requires knowledge of the demand function. In textbook examples, the monopolist charges the profit-maximizing price where marginal revenue equals marginal costs. Still, he may not know the demand function for his products (and probably also not the cost function). Informational requirements are enormous: even a simple linear demand function requires knowledge of at least two price–quantity coordinates, but these cannot be found in a trial and error process. Once the price is lowered, it may be challenging to return to a higher price.

The assumed strong tendency to equilibrium could be illustrated by the common use of the bell curve, where the probability of extreme deviations is low. Although with the bell curve, extreme events are unlikely, they nevertheless may happen. Taleb (2007) argues that the thin tails of the bell curve are underestimating the "extreme events," events away from the mean and writes:

> If there are strong forces of equilibrium bringing things back rather rapidly after conditions diverge from equilibrium, then again you can use the Gaussian approach. [...] This is why much of economics is based on the notion of equilibrium: among others benefits, it allows you to treat economic phenomena as Gaussian. (236)

In a dynamic economy, however, the "thin tails" where the black swans are, is still a centered concept, an equilibrium concept, with a constant normal. In a dynamic economy, the distributions are constantly shifting. In short, all evaluations of risk on past events (history) are inadequate and do not apply.

3. Rational choice: a normative concept

"Rational choice" is not descriptive of actual behavior but rather a prescriptive, normative concept deduced from a set of conditions classified as evident (axioms), representing the knowledge base. Choosing rationally requires an enormous amount of information, selection, and processing capacity, probably too much RAM for the human brain. Simon (1955, 1978, 1982) famously argued that the human brain could not evaluate all possible choices (endogenous constraints), bring them in a transitive order, and evaluate the consequences of choices (bounded rationality). Humans have limited information and lack the computational capacity to evaluate all alternatives and consequences. Rationality is bounded, and humans may target satisfying aspirations rather than aiming for the maximum. New York cab drivers who can determine their working hours illustrate the point: Instead of maximizing income on busy days, they stop working once they have reached their income target (Camerer et al. 1997).[1] Furthermore, unbiased perception of *the world we live in* is assumed: The map is the landscape?[2]

Behavior deviating from this rationality norm is often—even among those critical of "rational choice"— classified as "irrational," a mistake, an anomaly, or a paradox. Thaler (2015) nicely illustrated the dominance of "rational choice" in economics when he titled his book on the development of Behavioral Economics *Misbehaving*. Rational decision theories are based on optimization, calculating outcomes, whereas "non-rational" theories are not. Still, they should not be confused with the theories of "irrational" decision-making, but they simply follow different pro-

---

[1]   Winter-Ebner (2014) argues that taxi drivers are not representative of all workers. True, they are among the few workers with flexible enough working hours to test the aspiration level hypothesis.

[2]   Neuropsychologist Jäncke (2015) argues that the brain focuses on specific aspects eliminating others (functional blindness) illustrated with the gorilla crossing the screen unnoticed by the audience.

cedures (Gigerenzer 2001). Even if an optimizing strategy exists [if an expected value (utility) can be computed], it requires an unrealistic amount of information and processing capacity about the alternative options and the consequences of actions. "Indeed, nonrational theories are concerned with psychological plausibility, that is, the capacities and limitations of actual humans, whereas rational theories have little concern for descriptive validity and tend to assume omniscience" (Gigerenzer & Selten 2001: 3). History and habits (reference points) will change preferences. People rely on a limited number of heuristic principles which simplify the complex tasks of assessing probabilities and predicting values (Kahneman 2002: 465). Accepting incomplete knowledge and emotional factors that influence decisions of macroeconomic phenomena (e.g., instability) or self-enforcing the ups and downs, or the "roller-coaster ride" of the economy (Akerlof & Shiller 2009), is based on the microeconomic effects self-inferring each other.

All decisions are future-oriented, and their outcomes depend on the combination of preferences and the probabilities of their occurrence. Then "rational choice" asserts that humans maximize the product of the two components, adding another unknown variable to the maximization problem. Allais (1953) analyzed whether informed humans (those who understand probability theory) choose consistently under known probabilities not influenced by irrelevant alternatives. His experiment became known as Allais' paradox which is, Allais (1998) explains, only a paradox given the axioms of rational choice. Preferences may be known (the individual knows best), but do individuals know the probabilities related to the alternatives under uncertainty? The surprising answer was yes, "subjective probability": the probability the individual must have assumed if the observed choice maximizes utility. Subjective expected utility, or SEU, illustrates the axiomatic approach of neoclassical economics. Ellsberg (1961) designed an experiment explicitly investigating the consistency of subjective probability—the Savage axiom—and found that it fails. "Utility theory has nevertheless proven to be remarkably resilient to the experimental evidence that has accumulated against it" (Einhorn & Hogarth 1986: S226). However, assuming coherence in human decision-making is attractive because the laws of probability seem to make violation implausible (Tversky & Kahneman 1983), but that assumes knowledge of the alternatives and their probabilities. "We are merely reminding ourselves that human decisions affecting the future, whether personal or political or economic, cannot depend on a strict mathematical expectation, since the basis for making such calculations does not exist [...]" (Keynes 1936: 162–163).

3.1 PSYCHOLOGY VS. MATHEMATICS: BERNOULLI'S SOLUTION TO THE PETERSBURG PARADOX

In the 18th century, Nicolas Bernoulli[3] confronted his cousin Daniel Bernoulli (1738, 1954)[4] with a problem known as the "Petersburg Paradox." With an indefinite expected value, no reasonable person was expected to place a large bet in this game. If an ideal coin is tossed and payoffs double with every consecutive "head," the game's expected value is indefinite.[5] Because no reasonable person would bet a large amount on winning, Bernoulli argued that wealthier people would be prepared to risk higher sums than the less affluent. This led him to conclude that it is not the expected value (e.g., the product of payoff and probability) but the expected utility that guides decisions: "[...] in their theory, mathematicians evaluate money in proportion to its quantity while, in practice, people with common sense evaluate money in proportion to the utility they can obtain from it" (Bernoulli 1738, 1954: 33). Bernoulli brought the psychological value of money (now called utility, Kahneman 2011: 272) into economics and constructed his famous utility function with the declining marginal utility of wealth (income, respectively).[6] In short, the change in utility of monetary gains and losses depends on the wealth already achieved; it is valued relative to wealth.

---

[3]   The Bernoulli family includes many well-known mathematicians such as Jackob Bernoulli to whom the discovery of the law of large numbers is ascribed (see Fröba and Wassermann 2007).

[4]   The reference used is the translation of Bernoulli's paper published in *Econometrica* (1954), Vol. 21, No.1, pp. 22–36.

[5]   The probability of "head" is $\frac{1}{2}$ in the first toss, for two consecutive "heads" it is $\frac{1}{4}$ and for the nth toss it is $\frac{1}{2}^n$. The probability of wining declines with n but the value of payoffs increases with the number of tosses (2^{n-1}), so that after nth toss it adds $1/2^n * 2^{n-1} = \frac{1}{2}$ ducats, i.e., each toss adds the payoff times the probability of "head." The sum of gains is $\frac{1}{2}+\frac{1}{2}+\frac{1}{2}+ \ldots = $ indefinite ascribed to Menger (Footnote 9 in the translation of Bernoulli's paper (Bernoulli 1954, page 31).

However, with an upfront payment (a fee to participate) the first round expected gain is <=0!

[6]   A linear function is transformed into logarithmic function.

This relation also explains why reservation prices of wealthier people are higher than those of the less wealthy (Ironmonger 2000). It makes income (or wealth) the most relevant variable for price discrimination. Well-off people buy the "gold edition," and everyone else chooses the "home edition," even though the software is often identical (see Hassink & Schettkat 2003). Based on his concave utility function (Figure 3.1), Bernoulli argued that "... everyone who bets any part of his fortune, however small, on a mathematically fair game of chance acts irrationally, it may be of interest to inquire how great an advantage the gambler must enjoy over his opponent in order to avoid any expected loss" (Bernoulli 1738,1954: 29).[7] Usually, organized gambling is mathematically unfair, shifting the odds in favor of the organizer, such as the game of roulette.[8] Nevertheless, gambling may be fun, providing direct utility (as do many other activities, see Scitovsky 1976) aside from the prospective gains or addictions. Games may even be purposefully designed to get people hooked on them (Akerlof & Shiller 2015).[9]

Bernoulli argued that the risk is evaluated by the change in utility rather than by the change in wealth. His utility function implies that gains in wealth are perceived in utility terms less severe than similar losses in wealth. Left of point B in Figure 3.1 (where the function is steeper than to the right of B), a slight decline in wealth (dW-) leads to the same absolute loss in utility (dU-) as the more significant gain (dW+) leads to a rise in utility (dU+). Gains and losses in wealth are perceived differently in utility terms, but pecuniary gains can be observed directly, unlike utility which depends on perception and remains unmeasured. Using the logarithm of wealth as the utility function, as Peters and Gell-Mann

---

[7]   The utility function is also used to illustrate risk aversion (the concave function), neutrality (a linear function) or a hyperbolic function (risk seeking).

[8]   The chance of winning when setting on a number in roulette is 1/37, but the payoff is only 36 times the betted amount, i.e., the payout-probability combination is biased in favor of the casino.

[9]   In games, probabilities are defined, they are known or can be derived and for repeated games the law of large numbers applies for the ensemble (see Chapter 5.4). In *the world we live in*, however, events are seldom repeated and the economic environment changes continuously. Therefore probabilities are unknown. Even if constant probabilities underlie economic processes it is an heroic assumption that individuals can discover probabilities. Anyway, even if expected values can be computed, the next draw's outcome will result in a gain or a loss for the individual (for a discussion relevant for insurance issues, see Barr 2001, Peters & Gell-Mann 2016).

(2016) suggest, does not simply transform the wealth function but leads
to a measure of utility. However, the relative evaluation of changes to
initial wealth (expressed in the logarithmic function) seems plausible.
How changes in wealth are perceived inspired Kahneman and Tversky to
develop prospect theory, which stresses the importance of the direction of
changes in wealth for the perception of utility.

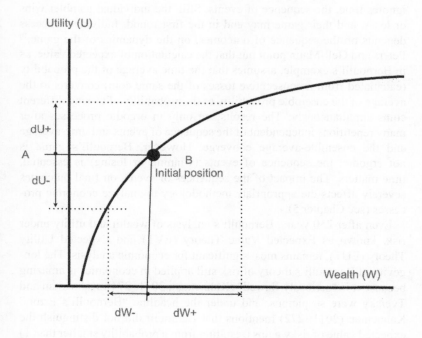

$$dU+ = |dU-| \; ; \; dW+ > |dW-|$$

Source: Graph inspired by Bernoulli (1738, 1954).

Figure 3.1   Risk in Bernoulli's utility function

Bernoulli's concave utility function implies that an increase in utility
requires a higher raise in wealth than the same absolute decline in utility.
In other words, losses hurt more than the enjoyment of gains.

3.2   BERNOULLI'S ERRORS I: PROSPECT THEORY

Physicists Peters and Gell-Mann (2016) are uncomfortable with Bernoulli's reference to "weak psychology," but not with Bernoulli's logarithmic function. However, the most critical point in their critique is that the widely applied calculation of expected value in economics ignores time, the sequence of events. Still, the individual gambler wins or loses, and their game may end in the first round. Individual success depends on the sequence of outcomes, on the dynamics of the game.[10] Peters and Gell-Mann point out that the calculation of expected value, as in Bernoulli's example, assumes that the time average of the probability (calculated from n consecutive tosses of the same coin) converts to the average of the ensemble probability or the probability of tossing different coins simultaneously. The results are only in ergodic processes after many repetitions independent of the sequence of events and time-average and the ensemble-average converge. However, Bernoulli's game is not ergodic; the sequence of events (winning or losing) is essential, time matters. The impact of the sequences of events on final outcomes severely affects the appropriate methodology to analyze economic processes (see Chapter 5).

Even after 250 years, Bernoulli's analysis of wealth and utility under risk, known as Expected Value Theory (EVT) and Expected Utility Theory (EUT), remains most significant for economic analysis. The longevity of Bernoulli's theory of risk still applied in economics is amazing because it is "seriously flawed" (Kahneman, 2011: 274). Kahneman and Tversky were suspicious, and under the headline "Bernoulli's Error," Kahneman (2011: 272) mentions that Bernoulli did not distinguish the expected value of risky gains (resulting from a probability smaller than 1) from the "sure thing." When choosing among gambles, people generally prefer the lower but sure gain over a somewhat higher but risky payoff (see Chapter 3.3 Allais' and Chapter 4.2 Ellsberg's "Paradoxes"). "We were not trying to figure out the most rational or advantageous choice; we wanted to find the intuitive choice [...]" (Kahneman 2011: 271). In their

---

[10]   Peters (2019) demonstrates that a random process, such as Bernoulli's game, should not be judged by the average expected gain. The average is composed of few winners with very high gains but many "losers" with low or no gains. In other words, the median is much lower than the average affected by the outlier (see Chapter 5.6).

prospect theory, Kahneman and Tversky criticize a basic assumption in neoclassical economics: the orientation on real values and the unbiased perception of situations. EUT is based on real wealth, but humans do not recognize simply the real wealth but also changes in their position compared to a reference point, usually the present position. Not only the level of perceived wealth (utility) but instead changes in wealth from a reference point affect utility. It makes a substantial difference in the perception of the utility of $1000 depending on the reference point. If the difference is negative (if there was a decline in wealth), the perception of the change in utility is substantially different from a positive difference: an increase in wealth. Humans evaluate (perceive) their situation depending on the reference point, which can be regarded as a form of habit formation (see Figure 3.2).

People's utility not only depends on the final level of wealth, as Bernoulli's utility function suggests but also (even more) on the changes in wealth. Kahneman offers an example: "Today, Jack and Jill each have a wealth of 5 million. Yesterday, Jack had 1 million, and Jill had 9 million. Are they equally happy? Do they have the same utility?" (Kahneman 2011: 275). At Bernoulli's utility function, Jill and Jack are at the same level of wealth, and they should be equally happy, but Jack experienced a 400% increase in wealth, whereas Jill suffered a 45% loss.[11] Even without a degree in psychology, one knows that Jack will be happy, and Jill will be unhappy if not desperate. Prospect theory emphasizes the change rather than the final stock of wealth to influence utility (happiness). The severe negative utility impact of losses is found, for instance, in wage schedules and fits the observed employers' avoidance of wage cuts (Bewley 1995, Solow 1979). However, Bernoulli argued that losses reduce utility more than gains increase utility along with his concave utility function. Indeed, the initial wealth position will affect the utility, and Kahneman and Tversky (1984) argue that the effect is even more substantial than Bernoulli's utility function implies. It is a psychological effect. The "value function" conceptualizes prospect theory. Most importantly, the function is steeper on the left (for losses) than on the right (for gains) of the reference point, but the slope of the curves diminishes to both ends.

---

[11] As the saying of speculators at the stock exchange goes, you can win 1,000% but you cannot lose more than 100%.

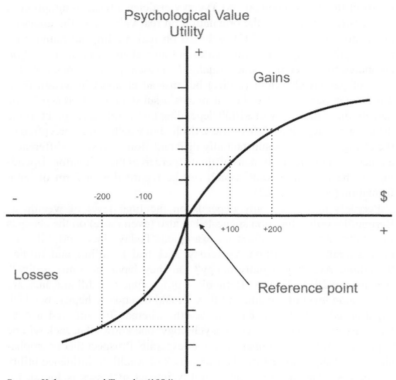

Source: Kahneman and Tversky (1984).

Figure 3.2   The psychological value function

Gains and losses are evaluated from a reference point (usually the status quo). The direction of change affects the psychological value not only the wealth as Bernoulli suggests.

True, Bernoulli's utility function suggests that similar levels of wealth lead to equal levels of utility (happiness). Kahneman and Tversky (1984) emphasize that the reference to absolute wealth is insufficient (Bernoulli's error) because the decline in utility from a loss weights more substantially than the reduced wealth position suggests. Losses in wealth are amplified in terms of utility. Still, the distinction between the utility derived from gains and losses is the core of Bernoulli's analysis of risk supported by his argument that participation even in mathematically fair games is irrational. However, Bernoulli missed the impact of the "sure thing," that certain payments are preferable to the expected value (Kahneman 2011: 275). However, Kahneman is correct that Bernoulli did not emphasize the psychological impact of changes in wealth sufficiently, but he certainly recognized the asymmetric utility effects of gains and losses. Although Bernoulli was not a behavioral economist, he surely was aware of the negative utility effect of losses; he missed the psychological impact of the relevance of reference points. In prospect theory, Kahneman and Tversky (1984) enhanced the importance of the "reference point," which implies that historical time and past decisions affect the current evaluations of prospective changes. In other words, the orientation on reference points is not compatible with stable preferences.

3.3 SWITCHING PREFERENCES: ALLAIS' "PARADOX"

That individuals know their stable preferences, that they rank all possible alternatives consistently, and choose the utility-maximizing option are the conditions for "rational choice." Which choices provide the highest utility may differ between individuals but the same person should make consistent choices not affected by framing or irrelevant additions (independence axiom). Transitivity requires if A is to be preferred over B and B over C, then A is preferred over C [A > B > C]. The addition of X to all choices should not affect the ranking. In other words, (A+X) > (B+X) > (C+X) because X cancels out in the comparison. These, however, are the requirements to behave according to the axioms of "rational choice," which is prescriptive. It is another issue of how individuals actually act. Do humans follow the rationality axioms? Are their choices "rational," are they consistent? Do individuals switch the decision criteria?

Friedman famously argued that theories could only be judged by comparing their predictions with actual results, but we do not observe whether the observed choices actually maximize utility. This is deduced from the maximizing axiom; if the axiom holds, observed choices must be maximizing utility. Allais (a French mathematical economist who was awarded the Nobel Prize in economics in 1988 "for his pioneering contributions to the theory of markets and efficient utilization of resources," Nobel Committee) tested "rational choice" in an experiment designed to investigate whether knowledgeable persons (those who understand decision theory) behave rationally in situations where probabilities are known (risk) and can be applied to evaluate choices: to investigate whether choices are consistent in maximizing expected values. In Allais' experiment, the same participants chose between two games in two different situations. In situation 1, the choice was between a sure win (game A) compared to a substantially higher payoff (game B), but a slight chance (1%) of no gain (displayed in the upper panel of Table 3.1). Allais observed that most persons chose game A (the sure but lower payoff) over B, where a lower but guaranteed payment is preferred to a higher but slightly risky gain (a higher gain but a 1% chance of no win). In situation 2, the same persons could choose between game C with a probability of 0.11 to win the lower sum and game D with a slightly lower probability of 0.10 to win the substantially higher sum. For the other cases (0.89, 0.90 probability), the gain was zero. Now, the same persons decided overwhelmingly for game D over game C. So in situation 2, the high but less likely win in game D is preferred to the lower but highly likely win in game C.

The participants in Allais' experiment violated the independence axiom that irrelevant additions should not affect the "rational choice": the preferences in situations 1 and 2 should be consistent. Consistency requires choosing either A and C or B and D, but combinations of A and D or B and C are inconsistent; they violate "rational choice." Indeed, the equivalences of games A and C and B and D are not easy to detect for a layperson and actually not for experts in decision theory. The middle panel of Table 3.1 displays the rearranged probabilities to see the equivalence. The 0.90 probability for a zero gain in game D can be split into a 0.89 (grey box in Table 3.1) plus a 0.01 chance. Since the alternative choice (game C) also has a 0.89 chance of a zero gain, these probabilities are irrelevant for the decision between games D and C, only the probabilities of winning 100 mill. or 500 mill. should be relevant.

Similarly, the probabilities in games A and B can be disentangled. Again, there is a 0.89 chance of winning the same amount in both games (grey-shaded boxes), which is irrelevant for choosing between the alternatives. Consolidating, the lower panel of Table 3.1 reveals that games A and C and B and D are identical. Therefore, "rational choice" (consistency) requires that if A is preferred to B in situation 1, to be consistent, the same persons must choose C over D in situation 2, or if B is preferred to A in situation 1, the choice must be D over C in situation 2. Switching from A over B in situation 1 to D over C in situation 2 or from B over A in situation 1 to C over D in situation 2 reveals a change of preferences, which violates the "rational choice" axioms and need to be declared "irrational."

Table 3.1   Allais' experiment deciphered

Payoff	Situation 1		Situation 2	
	A	B	C	D
	Probability	Probability	Probability	Probability
0		0.01	0.89	0.90
100 mill.	1.00	0.89	0.11	
500 mill.		0.10		0.10
Expected gain	100 mill.	139 mill.	11 mill.	50 mill.

Rearranged:

Payoff	Situation 1		Situation 2	
	A	B	C	D
	Probability	Probability	Probability	Probability
0			0.89	0.89
		0.01		0.01
100 mill.	0.89	0.89		
	0.11		0.11	
500 mill.		0.10		0.10

Consolidated:

Payoff	Situation 1		Situation 2	
	A	B	C	D
	Probability	Probability	Probability	Probability
0		0.1		0.1
100 Mill.	0.11		0.11	
500 Mill.		0.10		0.10

Source: Data from Allais (1953: 527). Empty cells represent probability = 0.

Most (knowledgeable) individuals switch the decision criteria from a secure payoff (A) to a high payoff (D) in what has become known as the "Allais paradox." However, Allais (1998) does not view these findings as a paradox because the observed behavior corresponds to the fundamental psychological reality that people switch the decision criteria from highest probability to highest value. The choices are paradoxical only if stable preferences and internal consistency of choices are assumed. One may argue that it is challenging to identify the games' outcomes and that it requires expertise in decision theory. True, but Allais not only consulted knowledgeable persons, but at a conference, he confronted the most distinguished economics professors and experts of decision theory with his experiment, among them Friedman, Samuelson, Savage, and Arrow (Kahneman 2011: 312–314). Even these distinguished experts switched preferences, as did people less well-versed in decision theory, not noticing that their expressed preferences violated *rational choice*. Savage (1954, according to Machina 1987) conceded that he violated the independence axiom when first confronted with Allais' experiment. After reflection, he corrected his initial choices to fit the independence axiom (see Starmer 2004).[12] In their paper "Who Accepts Savage's Axiom?" Slovic and Tversky (1974) report similar results of their experiments with a group of senior managers following Allais' and Ellsberg's (see below) examples. After explaining to the participants that they had made inconsistent choices that violated the fundamental axioms of neoclassical decision theory (rational choice), participants nevertheless kept their choices. The observed choices were no mistakes but expressing genuine preferences. However, the actual economy is more complex than games. Most humans are not experts in decision theory. Most importantly, it is unclear whether the economy follows the laws of probability. Even if it were, the probabilities might be unknown for the individual or likely irrelevant.

Obviously, ordinary people and experts in decision theory prefer lower but certain payoffs to higher ones with a slight probability of a zero payoff. Participants in the experiments did not adhere to the axiom of rationality, and therefore their choices cannot be attributed to maximizing along with a stable utility function. This is not just the reaction of layper-

---

[12]   Hirshleifer and Riley (1992) argue that Allais' finding only represents a logical lapsus, a rational person having been "tricked" by Allais' framing. If it were systematic failure, someone could exploit it (1992: 37–38).

sons who do not understand the inconsistency in their choices because distinguished scholars in decision theory also violated the rationality axiom. Kahneman (2011) explains the switch to lower but certain payoff in terms of the certainty effect: The negative utility effect of even a tiny deviation from certainty overcompensates the utility gain of a much higher payoff. That may make decisions sensitive to their presentation. This holds for a situation where the probabilities are known although not easily identified, but it is impossible to calculate probabilities in cases of uncertainty. Kahneman (2011) mentions that Allais' paradox was dismissed as an anomaly, with rationality remaining the standard assumption in economics. Forgotten or ignored? Allais' conference paper was published in *Econometrica* only after discussions among the "[...] prominent contributors to this field of study [...]" (Frisch 1953: 503, Editor's note in Allais 1953) and exchanges and revisions between Allais and the editor. At that time, Ragnar Frisch, the editor-in-chief, finally decided to publish the work, but only with an unusual editor's note mentioning Allais' responsibility for the paper and the editor's intention to prevent inbreeding of thoughts. In his contribution to the *New Palgrave*, Allais (1998: 82) blamed "[...] a dogmatic and intolerant, powerful and tyrannical domination over the academic world [...]" for delaying scientific progress.

3.4   BOUNDED RATIONALITY

Simon stressed that external and internal constraints make "rational choice" a theoretical construct because such an enormous amount of information exceeds the human brain capacity. Even if the motivation is profit or utility maximization, humans cannot reach that target; the decision process would be overly complex, and rationality is necessarily bounded. Humans follow "procedural rationality," meaning they rely on incomplete reasoning but do not simply follow impulses without reflection. If critics of rational choice argue that individuals do not follow the maximization axiom (motivation is broader) and cannot follow the decision procedures prescribed by the neoclassical model because of limited information collection and processing capacity, they are asserted to be naive. They are confronted with the astounding *as-if* response: Of course, "economic agents" do not literally perform the necessary steps in the ascribed decision process. Still, they behave *as-if* is the common defense of the theory by neoclassical economists in the past (Friedman 1953) and present (Pesendorfer 2006). Friedman famously illustrated the *as-if* ignorance with the example of a professional billiard player who does not perform the calculations necessary to give the balls the right direction and spin; they behave intuitively, *as-if*. Instead, decision procedures follow entirely different rules, meaning that humans apply various heuristics out of a toolbox in different situations (Gigerenzer & Selten 2001). Referring to Friedman's billiard player narrative, Gigerenzer illustrated the toolbox with a baseball fielder who does not behave *as-if*; he does not calculate a trajectory and the position where the ball will land. He uses gaze heuristic: He focuses the ball at a certain angle and keeps running, catching the ball at the proper position in the right moment (see the YouTube video Gigerenzer 2017). The two pilots, "Sully" Sullenberger and Jeffrey Skiles, who managed the emergency water landing of the US Airways jet known as the "Miracle on the Hudson" in 2009, also relied on gaze heuristics.

Defenders of the substantive rationality thesis argue that rational behavior—maximization—is enforced in competitive markets because only the most efficient survive. "Market discipline" purportedly enforces rational decisions, and repeated transactions will attenuate the discrepancies between optimizing and observed behavior (V. Smith 2002). Therefore, individual behavior is irrelevant; selection leads to the survival of the fittest, which is thought to be the maximizer. The assertion that the market imposes discipline on firms may hold in the perfect-market world, but hardly in *the world we live in* and not for people.

Bounded rationality emphasizes the constraints for decisions in the overly complex real-world even if probabilities are known. The SEU hypothesis frames the maximization problem as the product of subjective—guessed—probability and preference. Since individuals may have different preferences and probability guesses, the SEU thesis only requires consistent behavior, but even its leading proponents, Savage and Friedman, failed to decide accordingly. However, heuristics and intuitive decision-making may lead to decisions one would come to regret. However, as neurological research indicates, decisions require emotions that may be overruled after reflections, but purely rational thinking may never lead to any decision at all (Cohen 2005, Damásio 1994).

Berg and Gigerenzer's (2010) provocatively titled "As-If Behavioral Economics: Neoclassical Economics in Disguise?" criticizes Behavioral Economics for measuring actual decisions against (unsubstantiated) maximization. Diverging decisions are erroneous because the alternatives are not well understood due to someone's lack of intelligence and knowledge (probability theory) or the obviation of the efforts necessary to understand alternative options fully. Indeed, some contributions of Behavioral Economics assume that actual decisions are suboptimal because people cannot handle large amounts of information, do not understand probability theory, do not understand discounting, or a deviation between expected and experienced utility. Consequently, people may reconsider decisions and regret some of their decisions. Nevertheless, even if their motivation is maximization, they cannot follow the axiom. Frank (2008) clarifies that in Behavioral Economics, there are not only "departures from rational choice with regret" but also "departures from rational choice without regret" (82). A selfish but rational individual maximizing his utility would not tip in a restaurant they will never visit again, but most people do (although the amounts vary substantially by country). "People do not really think of the tip as an incentive for good service. [...] They felt an obligation to pay him. They had no regret" (Frank 2008: 84).

Can it be rational to give money away? The "obligation to tip" can be interpreted in different ways: It may be an additional argument in the utility function, which makes maximizing utility maybe even more complex. Being generous may be part of one's own identity (Akerlof & Kranton 2011). Similarly, other aspects of social life, like inequality altruism (see Fehr & Schmidt 1999, Becker 1993a) but also selfish arguments like reputation, buying future well-treatment, and so on, may be integrated, but the assumption of maximizing own utility remains. The decision process may follow procedures other than the "cold calculation" to maximize a utility function, as Gigerenzer and Selten (2001) emphasize. Behavioral Economics classifies deviant behavior in terms of departure from the neoclassical axioms. It suggests "ecological rationality" instead (i.e., the match between decision processes and the environments in which they are used).

Doctors thinking back and forth in the emergency room is impossible and does not lead to the best outcome if quick decisions are required. True, it does not exclude that the decisions may be regretted once time allows thinking the procedures over. This seems to be Kahneman's point when he argues that decisions made in system 1 (fast, automatic, associative) may be overruled or regretted after system 2 (the cognitive process) evaluated them. The intuitive system 1 does the fast, intuitive decision-making, whereas system 2 is slow but applies careful thinking and controls system 1. Kahneman illustrates the difference—as always in his remarkable work—contrasting the immediate, intuitive answer to problems with the reflected answer. For example, listen to intuition and solve this question: "A bat and a ball together cost $1.10. The bat costs one dollar more than the ball. How much does the ball cost? A number came to your mind. The number, of course, is 10: 10 cents" (Kahneman 2011: 44). However, according to the math (system 2), if the ball is 10 cents and the bat costs one dollar more, the sum is $1.20. The ball is 5 cents, and the bat is $1.05. The intuition was fast but wrong.

Remarkably, this distinction between system 1 and system 2 is reflected in neuroeconomics: the application of the neurosciences to economic decisions. System 1 seems to be the emotional decision procedure controlled and occasionally overruled by the cognitive region of the brain (Cohen 2005, Hsu et al. 2005).

4. Choice under uncertainty: animal spirits

4.1 SUBJECTIVE PROBABILITY, TRANSFORMING UNCERTAINTY INTO RISK?

"Rational Choice," the maximization of expected utility (value), depends on a clear understanding of probabilities and gains. In games, probabilities and payoffs are known, but in *the world we live in* uncertainty rather than known probabilities (risk), and uncertain payoffs are the rule. Complications arise from humans' sensitivity to contextual variables, and their changes strongly affect the evaluation of risk, and estimated probabilities seem to depend on payoffs (Einhorn & Hogarth 1986). "[…] when assessing uncertainty in real-world tasks, the precision of the gambling analogy can be misleading. Specifically, beliefs about uncertain events are typically loosely and ill defined" (Einhorn & Hogarth 1986: S229). Therefore, decision rules that depend on calculations are impossible to apply under uncertainty. Defending rational choice, the argument starts from the end when it is assumed that individuals base their decisions on "subjective expected utility" (SEU), which supposedly transforms uncertainty into risk. Subjective probability is a guess or a feeling, it can formally close the rational choice equation (below), but it remains a guess. How to decide if calculations are impossible? How to choose under uncertainty?

SEU is claimed to reduce uncertainty to risk. Still, it simply balances an equation with three unknown variables of which unobserved expected utility is assumed to be the maximum. SEU does not answer whether humans maximize and whether choices differ under uncertainty from those under risk. It clearly illustrates the axiomatic approach: If "rational humans" maximize SEU, their decisions must blend individual preferences and probability, which may be objectively known in some circumstances but are uncertain in others. In Savage's SEU approach, subjective probability makes choices compatible with the maximization assumption and transforms objective uncertainty into subjective risk. However, a fundamental premise of rational choice is that individuals make consistent choices. Therefore subjective probability should not change depending on framing.

Subjective probability is usually ascribed to Ramsey (1926), who distinguished formal from "human logic" entailing a subjective element: a degree of belief. If objective probabilities are unknown, individuals may nevertheless make consistent decisions depending on their own belief in subjective probability. Von Neumann and Morgenstern's (1944) *Theory of Games and Economic Behavior* stated that all uncertainties could be reduced to risks because the expected utility of a particular choice is the combination of preferences and probability. Assuming that the "rational man" is maximizing utility, observed choices reveal the individual's preferences for specific alternatives and the subjective probabilities of their occurrence. If choosing rationally, the rational individual must have assumed a probability when calculating expected utility, even under objectively unknown probabilities (uncertainty). Decisions under uncertainty are transformed into calculable choices under risk so that the decision seems subjectively "rational." SEU became influential through the papers of Friedman and Savage (1948, 1952). They emphasize that "The maximization of such an expected value [utility] may also be regarded as a maxim for behavior" (Friedman & Savage 1952: 463). They claim that SEU had wide-ranging consequences for economic theory.

Subjective probability makes a choice formally consistent ("rational"), but it remains a guess and should not be confused with the true probability. In essence, the concept formalizes choice with an equation that involves three unmeasured variables:

$$Ui(max) \quad = \quad Ui(preference) \quad * \quad Pi(preference)$$

Ui(max) unobserved, maximum asserted   =   *Ui(preference)* unobserved   *   *Pi(preference)* unobserved

Where $Ui(max)$ = individual's maximum utility for alternative i, $Ui(preference)$ = individual's expected utility derived from the preferred alternative i, $Pi(preference)$ = subjective probability for the preferred alternative i.

None of these variables is observed or measured. However, the axiomatic approach assumes that observed choices are utility-maximizing, declared rational. Therefore, the product on the right-hand side of the equation must be the highest among all alternatives because the left-hand side is deduced to be the maximum (deduced from the axioms). Therefore, the actual choice reveals the maximum utility of the product of preferences and probability. "The upshot of their consistency conditions on the consumer is that his numerical or cardinal probabilities and numerical or cardinal utilities can be said to be uniquely and simultaneously defined, with the numerical probabilities satisfying the usual algebraic laws" (Samuelson 1952: 670). The fact that a decision is made and that this decision is assumed to follow the maximization axiom means that the consumer must ascribe a probability to it. With the SEU hypothesis, observed choices are made logically consistent with the maximization axiom, but, of course, subjective probability cannot reveal unknown probabilities; it just creates consistency of the hypothesis introducing an unmeasured bet "as if." "[E]conomic research often seems to work backward from empirical findings to whatever utility maximization will work. Where the empirical arrow falls, there we paint the utility bullseye" (Conlisk 1996: 685).

Assuming coherence in decision-making "is attractive because the strong normative appeal of the laws of probability make its violation implausible" (Tversky & Kahneman 1983: 313). However, as Ellsberg showed, when laws of probability are "violated," humans may simply switch their decision criteria. Whereas perceptions may often be proven objectively through measurement, objective measurement of probability is often unavailable, "and most significant choices under risk require an intuitive evaluation of probability" (Tversky & Kahneman 1983: 313). In "Judgement under Uncertainty: Heuristics and Biases" Tversky and Kahneman (1974, see also Kahneman & Tversky 1972) describe several heuristics used to estimate probabilities such as representativeness (probability estimates affected by the degree of resemblance), availability (the ease of retrieving similar events from memory), adjustment and anchoring (adjusting probabilities from a starting point). In the last type of heuristics, adjustments are usually insufficient because the framing of the issue affects the probability estimate. In the case of representativeness, Tversky and Kahneman argue that the resemblance dominates knowledge of the base rate, which is the information on the prior probability. In their example, the resemblance of personal characteristics usually ascribed to librarians dominates the probability estimate that the randomly chosen person is a librarian ignoring the information on the composition of the population in which other occupations have much larger shares. Availability is helpful to estimate frequencies or probabilities because instances of large classes are usually recalled better because they are more familiar. However, they may be biased by recent events or personal experiences.

In general, probability estimates seem to be affected by the context and payoffs, which may change the weight given to uncertainty (Einhorn & Hogarth 1986) among naive and sophisticated subjects (Tversky & Kahneman 1983). Objective measurement of perceptions may often be possible, but the objective measurement of probability is usually unavailable. "In the absence of an objective criterion of validity, the normative theory of judgement under uncertainty has treated the coherence of belief as the touchstone of human rationality" (Tversky & Kahneman 1983: 313). When probabilities of conjunct events are involved, naive people seem to get the "math" wrong and ascribe to the conjunction a higher probability than the individual event. "The conjunction error demonstrates with exceptional clarity the contrast between the extensional logic that underlies most formal conceptions of probability and the natural assessments that govern many judgments and beliefs" (Tversky & Kahneman 1983: 310). Therefore, using heuristics is helpful to make probability estimates. However, they are likely biased, and subjective probability is sufficient to close the rationality equation, but almost certainly, it does not lead to probability estimates that are helpful in actual maximization. "Our studies of the conjunction rule show that normatively inspired theories that assume coherence are descriptively inadequate, whereas psychological analyses that ignore the appeal of normative rules are, at best, incomplete" (Tversky & Kahneman 1983: 313). Utility maximization is the unproven assumption, but preferences and subjective probabilities are certainly affected by other factors such as "analysis errors, myopic impulses, inattention, passivity, and misinformation, to name a few" (Beshears et al. 2008: 3).

Subjective probability is not an objective probability, but it is claimed that the former reduces uncertainty to subjective risk. The roulette player who puts all his money on red obviously assumes a high subjective probability for red, but the draw may discourage this belief. Is he rational? The logical consistency of a deduced theory is relevant, but as Marschak (1950) points out, certain maxims must also be descriptive. Neoclassical economics, however, is more concerned with the internal coherence of the axiomatic theory than with describing actual behavior. Friedman and Savage illustrate this point: "Confidence in the hypothesis derives largely from its coherence with the body of economic theory and, more important, from the plausibility of the postulates with which it can be shown to be equivalent rather than from repeated success in prediction" (Friedman & Savage 1952: 474). The coherence of the theory, consistent deductions is proof of the theory? The relevance of SEU does not depend "on its empirical verification for the economic behavior of men at large, but on its acceptability, to individuals who are particularly concerned with such decisions, as a rule guiding "wise" behavior in the face of uncertainty" (Friedman & Savage 1952: 463 footnote). In other words, the theory (SEU) is prescriptive rather than descriptive to *the world we live in*. Friedman and Savage confess that the hypothesis "should be rejected if its predictions are generally contradicted by observation" (Friedman & Savage 1952: 473), which are the observed choices declared to be maxima. Again, the process itself is not under review.

> However, it is our bet itself, and not the reasoning and evidence that lies behind it, that gives operational meaning to our statement that we find one outcome "more likely" than another. And we may be willing to place bets—thus revealing "degrees of belief" in a quantitative form—about events for which there is no statistical information at all, or regarding which statistical information seems in principle unobtainable. (Ellsberg 1961: 644)

4.2   TESTING SEU: THE ELLSBERG PARADOX[1]

Ellsberg[2] (1961) designed an experiment to test the impact of uncertainty on choices explicitly testing Savage's axiom, or SEU. Ellsberg designed his experiment as choices between different games to disentangle preferences from subjective probability and to analyze the consistency in subjective probability. The payoffs were held constant, so choices between the games should vary consistently with the ascribed subjective probability, if rational. "I propose to indicate a class of choice-situations in which otherwise reasonable people neither wish nor tend to conform to the Savage postulates, nor the other axiom sets that have been devised" (Ellsberg 1961: 646). Ellsberg (1961) designed his experiment to critique the assumption that uncertainty is transformed into risk. The experiment investigates the required consistency of probabilities individuals ascribe to outcomes under ambiguity, Ellsberg's wording for uncertainty.

---

[1]   Ellsberg's "ambiguity" is similar to Keynes' "uncertainty" or what Keynes (1921) had called "non-comparable probabilities."

[2]   Ellsberg had a remarkable and diverse career and got fame as a whistle-blower with the Pentagon Papers which made public that the US administration did not believe that the Vietnam war could not be won (see Wells 2016, *Wild Man*). His academic work was long forgotten and his dissertation was only published in 2001.

Table 4.1   Ellsberg's one-urn experiment

Choice between two games in two rounds from an urn with 1/3 red balls and 2/3 black and yellow balls in unknown proportion. One ball is drawn. All games offer a payoff of $100.

First round		Second round	
A: Red wins	B: Black wins	C: Red or yellow wins	D: Yellow or black wins
Majority chooses A		Majority chooses D	
Implied proportions for majority choice			
Black < 1/3	Black > 1/3	Black < 1/3	Black > 1/3

Source: Derived from Ellsberg (1961).

Ellsberg's urn experiment (1961: 650)[3] has two rounds. In each round, participants have to choose between two games. The ball is picked from an urn in which one-third of the balls are red, two-thirds are black and yellow in unknown proportions. Participants can choose between two games, each with a winning payoff of $100. In game A, the participant wins if the drawn ball is red, and they win in game B if the drawn ball is black. Since the payoffs are identical, the probability assigned to the outcomes should determine the expected gain, depending on the subjective probability of drawing a black ball in game B. The overwhelming majority of participants choose game A in the first round, with the known probability of red balls. This choice, however, implies that the subjective probability for a black ball must be one-third or less and that the subjective probability for a yellow ball is one-third or higher.

In the second round, participants again choose between two games from the same urn (same proportions and payoffs as in round 1). Now the player wins if the drawn ball is red or yellow (game C) and in the other choice (game D) if the ball is black or yellow. The majority of participants (same players) now choose game D. These choices—game A (red ball) but game D (black or yellow)—reveal inconsistent subjective prob-

---

[3]   The experiment is similar to Keynes' thought experiment for decisions under uncertainty published in his *Treatise on Probability* in 1921 but Ellsberg did not mention Keynes in his 1961 paper. Economic historians (Feduzi 2007, Sakai 2018, Zappa 2015) argue that Ellsberg simply overlooked the parallels to Keynes' work in his 1961 article but that he showed high respect to Keynes' work in his 1962 dissertation at Harvard (published only in 2001, Ellsberg 2001). However, "Presumably, such non-symmetrical treatment of Keynes by Ellsberg seemed to be mysterious to every conscientious reader" (Sakai 2018: 9).

abilities, a violation of rationality. Choosing game A in round 1 implies that the proportion of yellow balls in the urn is greater than one-third; the probability of drawing a red or yellow ball in round 2 should be expected to be higher than two-thirds. The choice pattern (A in round 1 but D in round 2) fails to fit Savage's axiom of consistent subjective probability.

Thus, Ellsberg's experiments of observed choices consistently violate the subjective probability hypothesis and contradict Savage's hypothesis that actual choices represent utility maximization under consistent subjective probability. In all cases, the utility derived from the expected monetary values is the same ($100), and variations must be due to subjective probability differences. The Ellsberg experiment demonstrates that the rational decision postulate, the SEU, does not hold. Simply put, ambiguity and uncertainty about the actual proportions of yellow and black balls affect the decision. What explains the switch from A to D? Ellsberg's experiment demonstrates uncertainty-aversion since the chances of winning in games A and D are known but not in B and C. Table 4.1 summarizes Ellsberg's experiment. Ellsberg concluded that human decisions suffer from an aversion to uncertainty.

Keynes also argued that humans avoid uncertainty and choose the alternative which provides additional information; they give these alternatives more weight. In his *Treatise on Probability* (Keynes 1921: 75–76), he proposed a thought experiment: One ball is drawn from different urns containing black and white balls (see Table 4.2). There is an equal number of black and white balls in the first urn, and this is known. In the second urn, the proportions of black and white balls are unknown and uncertain. Following Jacob Bernoulli's principle of non-sufficient reason (Shackle 1958), the best guess for the second urn is that half of the balls are white and half are black. Keynes argued that the additional information on equal proportions in urn 1 gives a choice for this urn a higher weight. Most importantly, the weight assigned to an outcome is independent of the probability, which remains 50% in both cases, but the additional information provides higher confidence (Keynes 1921: 75).

New evidence may raise or decrease the probability "[…] but *something* seems to have increased in either case—we have a more substantial basis upon which to rest our conclusion. I express this by saying that an accession of new evidence increases the *weight* of an argument" (Keynes 1921: 71, emphasis in original). Additional information may sometimes affect probability, but even if it leaves the probability unchanged, "[…] it will always increase its weight" (Keynes 1921: 71). Keynes argued that the weight in favor of drawing W is greater in case 1 than in case 2, which

Table 4.2   Keynes' example of choice under uncertainty

Urn 1	Urn 2
Black and white balls, 50%	Black and white balls, unknown proportions
Higher "weight."	

Source: Derived from Keynes (1921), 75–76.

would be in Ellsberg's language preference for the clear numerical case (see Sakai 2018). Kahneman (2011) simply translates Keynes' weight into a preference for more certain alternatives.

Hirshleifer and Riley (1992) regard Ellsberg's experiment as a fruitful activity for psychologists wishing to fool *homo oeconomicus* by framing but with little significance for economics. "We would go so far as to insist that rationality failures have no economic implications. If these shortcomings do indeed represent ways in which people could systematically be fooled, economists would predict that tricksters, confidence men, and assorted rogues would enter the "industry" offering such gambles to naive subjects" (Hirshleifer & Riley 1992: 34). Clearly, they believe in the power of markets driven by self-interested individuals leaving no option unused. The market achieves the optimum; if some individuals fail, the market will do.

Actually, framing seems to have an enormous effect on decisions, and indeed, ordering options are used to influence decisions. Certainly, humans make mistakes and regret wrong choices, but often choices seem to be taken without regret. *Nudge* (Thaler & Sunstein 2008) demonstrates the power of "soft paternalism." Akerlof and Shiller's (2015) *Phishing for Phools: the economics of manipulation and deception* is full of examples illustrating how "anchoring" is used to "phool" buyers: Coffee comes in small, medium or large, and—guess what—the medium is the most popular. The most expensive drink is listed first in coffee houses, giving the impression that it is better than the others (Taleb 2007). Phone contracts have low introductory rates for the first three months, and then prices are raised. "So the introduction of a reference point in the forecaster's mind will work wonders. This is no different from a starting point in a bargaining episode, […], the discussion will be determined by that initial level" (Taleb 2007: 159).

Ariely (2008) describes the power of anchoring: Testing the willingness to pay, subjects (managers and MIT students) were asked for the price they would pay for product A. The treatment group was asked for the last two digits of their social security number and then for their willingness to pay; the control group was asked for the willingness to pay directly. The higher the social security number, the higher the respondents' price was willing to pay. "Similarly, once we bought a new product at a particular price, we become anchored to that price. But how does this work? Why do we accept anchors?" (Ariely 2008: 25–26). The power of anchoring can also be demonstrated with a certain discount (say $7) for a cheap pen compared to the same saving for an expensive suit (Tversky & Kahneman 1981). Ariely emphasizes that anchoring has significant implications for economic theory. The willingness to pay indicates consumer preference or marginal utility (Marshall 1890), and the asking price reflects the marginal cost. If the willingness to pay can be easily manipulated, "this means that consumers don't, in fact, have a good handle on their own preferences and the prices they are willing to pay for different goods and experiences" (Ariely 2008: 45). The market-clearing price (the market equilibrium) is no longer determined by independent demand and supply functions but is manipulated. "In the real world, anchoring comes from manufacturer's suggested prices, advertised prices, promotion, product introduction, etc.—all of which are supply-side variables" (Ariely 2008: 45).

Under the SEU hypothesis, probabilities should affect decisions, but confidence—differing between risk and uncertainty—should not. Ellsberg's experiment, however, shows that decisions deviate under risk and uncertainty. Of course, payoffs are the other relevant component here, but Ellsberg controlled for payoffs by holding them constant. "This empirical aversion to ambiguity motivates a search for neural distinctions between risk and ambiguity" (Hsu et al. 2005: 1680). Hsu et al.'s paper explicitly relates to Ellsberg's finding showing greater activity in response to uncertainty than in risky choice where probabilities are known. To control for the action and interaction between different brain regions, neurologists select into their samples people with lesions in specific brain regions; this way, controlling the impact of the regions.

Hsu et al. (2005) apply functional magnetic resonance brain imaging methods (fMRI) to investigate brain responses in decision-making under uncertainty and risk. They find that uncertainty "[...] correlates positively with activation in the amygdala and orbitofrontal cortex, and negatively with a striatal system" (Hsu et al., 2005: 1680). The orbitofrontal cortex is active in cognitive decision-making, whereas the amygdala (the evolutionary oldest part of our brain, Cohen 2005) is hypothesized to be the general vigilance module as part of the limbic system, which is related to emotions. Patients with impaired functioning of the orbitofrontal cortex were risk- and uncertainty-neutral, whereas subjects without that lesion appeared to be risk- and uncertainty-averse. "Neurological subjects with orbitofrontal lesions were insensitive to the level of ambiguity and risk in behavioral choices. These data suggest a general neural circuit responding to degrees of uncertainty, contrary to decision theory" (Hsu et al., 2005: 1680). Choices can vary substantially depending on the information of outcome probabilities, but SEU assumes no difference in risk and uncertainty situations. "Our results show that this is wrong on both the behavioral and neural level, and suggest a unified treatment of ambiguity and risk as limiting cases of general system evaluation uncertainty" (Hsu et al. 2005: 1683). In other words, decisions involve emotions.

4.3   SUBJECTIVE PROBABILITY OR ANIMAL SPIRITS?

In *the world we live in*, the informational base of future-oriented decisions is at best risky or more likely uncertain. How to decide under uncertainty when objective probabilities are unknown? Since decisions on investments and consumption are made, humans must have some vision of the future. Although objective probabilities are unknown, following the "formal logic" (Ramsey 1926) and calculating "objective" expected utility, "human logic" (Ramsey 1926) allows estimating subjective expected utility. "Human logic," however, simply leads to a guess of probability that allows balancing the equation of three unobserved variables. It formally establishes the consistency of individual decisions. However, it remains a belief, a guess based on human perceptions and intuition. It is not magic. Although SEU was celebrated in economic theory, it says nothing about how humans make the probability guess. Maximization of utility is the assumed behavior; that is what people do; it does not need any evidence or investigation for human motivation.

Do individuals behave rationally if they follow their guesses of probabilities? Is it irrational not to guess a probability? If rational behavior simply means to follow a set of axioms, subjective probability assures logical consistency. Still, it depends on unmeasured variables: is the utility maximum actually achieved, is the subjective probability consistently estimated? This approach to defining rational choice is self-referencing because it cannot be disproven as long as subjective utility, preferences, and subjective probability remain unmeasured. Given the celebration of SEU maximization under guessed probability (subjective probability) as the cornerstones of rational choice, it is astonishing that so many economists cannot accept animal spirits as a solution for decisions under unknown probabilities.

If decisions under uncertainty must be made, they must follow a different procedure. Keynes' shortcut for emotions and moods finally affecting decisions is *animal spirits* which are the basis for economic decisions under uncertainty. Moods, optimism or pessimism, lead to the final push to decide because, under uncertainty, no rational decisions can be made. Cold calculations cannot bring decisions about. "Thus if the *animal spirits* are dimmed and the spontaneous optimism falters, leaving us to depend on nothing but a mathematical expectation, enterprise will fade and die; though fears of loss may have a basis no more reasonable than hopes of profit had before" (Keynes 1936: 162). Keynes emphasizes conventional behavior (routine, heuristics) as an essential decision rule under uncertainty. Traditional behavior or traditional method of calculation assumes "[…] that the existing state of affairs will continue indefinitely, except insofar as we have specific reasons to expect a change" (Keynes 1936: 152). These routines are applied in most companies and developed over time (Nelson & Winter 1982) and probably become standard after a while. Routines may be regarded as habits based on experience, and knowledge plays a crucial role in current decisions. If knowledge under uncertainty is always incomplete and investment decisions need to be made in the real world, some other decision rules must be applied. Keynes labeled these *animal spirits* in the *General Theory*, indicating a necessity to action without calculating all options' outcomes.

> Most, probably, of our decisions to do something positive, the full consequences of which will be drawn out over many days to come, can only be taken as a result of *animal spirits*—of a spontaneous urge to action rather than inaction, and not as the outcome of a weighted average of quantitative benefits multiplied by quantitative probabilities. (Keynes 1936: 161)

Expectations are the basis for endogenous economic instability in Keynes' theory, as Akerlof and Shiller (2009) emphasized. Accepting emotional factors influencing decisions and macroeconomic phenomena (e.g., instability) or self-enforcing the ups and downs, or the "roller coaster ride" of the economy (Akerlof & Shiller 2009: 1), is based on the microeconomic effects self-inferring each other.[4] Akerlof and Shiller (2009) use *animal spirits* to encompass all irrational behavior or *non-rational expectations*. It is difficult to think about economic decisions, which are not *non-rational*, since the conditions for *rational expectations*, or calculable risks, are hardly ever fulfilled. Therefore, decisions must be based on spontaneity, whether labeled animal spirits or subjective probability. Neither of which can make uncertainty disappear, but animal spirits do not claim to do so. Shiller (2021) argues along similar routes as Minsky (1977, 1992) that spontaneous optimism or animal spirits may be contagious under uncertainty. Contagion of viruses and ideas is based on individuals' interaction but assumed away in methodological individualism.

The relevance of animal spirits is discussed controversially. Emotions, mood, spontaneous optimism or pessimism, animal spirits are for many economists (even among those who classify themselves Keynesians) difficult to accept because the rational choice hypothesis dominates economics, and relaxing it creates fear of losing the scientific nimbus. For example, Barens (2011) accuses Akerlof and Shiller's book (2009) of overemphasizing *animal spirits* when they want to build a new economics on this concept. Barens states that *animal spirits* are mentioned only three times in the *General Theory* and only on one or two pages. This is accurate, but counting words may not be the best way of judging the relevance of Keynes' arguments. Many passages of the *General Theory* and especially Keynes' 1937 reply to comments on the *General Theory* show that he saw animal spirits as essential for decisions under uncertainty, supported by recent findings of neurologists. "Even apart from the instability due to speculation, there is the instability due to the characteristic of human nature that a large proportion of our positive activities depend on spontaneous optimism rather than on a mathematical expectation, whether moral or hedonistic or economic" (Keynes 1936: 161). Keynes adds: "Enterprise only pretends to itself to be mainly actuated by the statements in its own prospectus, however candid and sincere" (Keynes 1936: 161–162). Keynes emphasizes conventional behavior (routines, heuristics) as an essential decision rule under uncertainty. Thus, Keynes recognized that experience, knowledge, and habit formation are crucial

---

[4]   For positive feedback effects see Arthur (1994a), Young (1928), and Chapter 5.

in current decisions. Whatever the labels, today's choices cannot be rational.[5]

Schumpeter used entrepreneurial leadership and intuition, Keynes referred to *animal spirits*. Although based on feelings, on the desire to do rather than pure reflection, Schumpeter's entrepreneurial spirits were perceived as a clever, risk-taking way to chase prospective profits. "But they were not contrasted with the interests and were rather assumed to be one of their manifestations" (Hirschman 1992: 50). *Animal spirits* affecting decisions are not irrational in the sense that decisions are just based on moods.

> We should not conclude from this that everything depends on waves of irrational psychology. On the contrary, the state of long-term expectation is often steady, and, even when it is not, the other factors exert their compensating effects. We are merely reminding ourselves that human decisions affecting the future, whether personal or political or economic, cannot depend on strict mathematical expectation, since the basis for making such calculations does not exist; and that it is our innate urge to activity which makes the wheels go round, our rational selves choosing between the alternatives as best we are able, calculating where we can, but often falling back for our motive on whim or sentiment or chance. (Keynes 1936: 162–163)

Animal spirits are similar to conventions and heuristics, which help to decide in situations of uncertainty where "cold calculations" will not do. Emotions influence our decisions whether we acknowledge it or not (Cohen 2005). Neurological research led to a conception of the human brain as a confederation of mechanisms whose activity can be observed with new non-invasive methods like functional magnetic resonance imaging (fMRI), enabling "substantial progress in understanding the neural mechanisms underlying emotional and cognitive processes" (Cohen 2005: 8).

Neurologist Damásio's (1994) impressive work shows that people cannot decide without emotions or animal spirits. The fascinating discovery of Damásio starts with Phineas Gage, a construction foreman for a railroad company in Vermont. In 1848, his skull was perforated by an iron tamping rod during an explosion. "The iron enters Gage's

---

[5] A paper on the origin of Keynes' concept of *animal spirits* in the *Journal of Economic Perspectives* (Koppl 1991) led several economic historians to wonder whether or not Descartes had inspired Keynes to use this term, even citing the notes Keynes had taken as a student.

left cheek, pierces the base of the skull, traverses the front of his brain, and exits at high speed through the top of the head" (Damásio 1994: 4). Although Gage survived the accident and was pronounced healed after a few months, but "[…] Gage was no longer Gage […]" (Damásio 1994: 7). He was restless and had difficulties making decisions. Reconstruction of Phineas' brain and skull made possible through modern techniques led to the conclusion that his prefrontal cortices suppressed emotions, causing his endless reasoning. Damásio also observed similar characteristics in patients who suffered from injuries of their prefrontal cortices after surgery. They also continuously collect information and evaluate alternatives but hesitate to decide. Lerner et al. (2015) summarized their review of 35 years of research in emotions and decision-making that "[…] emotion and decision making go hand in hand" (801). "Indeed, many psychological scientists now assume that emotions are, for better or worse, the dominant driver of most meaningful decisions in life" (Lerner et al., 2015: 801). Different parts of our brain are involved in decision-making. Emotions are essential, but the cognitive system may override the limbic system, and sometimes the different regions of the brain may be in competition. This seems to be the conclusion of the fascinating neurological research on decision-making.

5. Expectations over time

5.1 IT'S NOT FOR US TO SEE WHAT THE FUTURE WILL BE

Time moves in one direction; today's economic actions will influence our constraints and options for tomorrow's decisions but not yesterday's. Most aspects of life suffer from intertemporal interdependence, although independence is often assumed. "It is this independence axiom that is crucial for the Bernoulli-Savage theory of maximization of expected cardinal utility" (Samuelson 1952: 672). Thus, wants, desires, opportunities, and constraints have a time component; they are dynamic instead of static. The *economy we live in* requires the recognition of intertemporal dependencies and sequential analysis.

Behavioral Economics emphasizes several intertemporal dependencies. A popular example is today's choice of a restaurant where Italian food yesterday may create a preference for Thai food today (i.e., a negative feedback effect). There is also a possibility of positive feedback; for instance, listening to classical music in the past may instill a desire to listen to it again in the future, developing a habit. Positive and negative feedback are essential whenever systems evolve, like technology or economies that change in a sequential process, characterized as cumulative causation (Myrdal 1957) or learning by using (Rosenberg 1994).[1] It is often argued that the market will pick the most advantageous technology, but this is by no means clear that the most efficient technology will dominate market processes (Arthur 1994a). The sequence of events is essential whenever positive feedback effects lead to non-ergodic processes. In ergodic processes, the sequence of events is unimportant. Comparing equilibria before and after an event—comparative statics—is

---

[1] Path dependence, lock-ins through network externalities are only two of many issues.

sufficient because the intermediate market process does not matter, at least not in the long run.

All decisions are future-oriented and based on expectations, but expected utility may differ from utility experienced later. In other words, recent decisions may affect future choices.

> This fact of one-at-a-time consumption does not carry the implication that f [the utility function] can be written in terms of additive independent functions of dated beer and dated milk. On the contrary, my relative desire for beer now generally depends upon how much beer and milk I consumed in the past and will consume in the future. (Samuelson 1952: 675)[2]

In Behavioral Economics and Keynes' theory, expectations are key. Again, neoclassical economics does not take time and expectations seriously: Preferences are presumably stable and form convex indifference curves. The neoclassical model is constructed so that diminishing returns and negative feedback dominate, ensuring ergodic development—a predictable economic environment, an equilibrium—but in the *economy we live in*, positive feedback effects are manifold. The rational expectations hypothesis rests on the assumption of a predictable, stable economic environment that is only vulnerable to exogenous shocks. Individuals know or have learned that solid market forces bring the economy back to essentially the former equilibrium position. Equating economics with the neoclassical model, Lucas (1986) argues:

> Economics has tended to focus on situations in which the agent can be expected to "know" or to have learned the consequences of different actions so that his observed choices reveal stable features of his underlying preferences. [...] Technically, I think of economics as studying decision rules that are steady states of some adaptive process, decision rules that are found to work over a range of situations and hence are no longer revised appreciably as more experience accumulates. (Lucas 1986: 218)

Thus, Lucas deliberately limits economics to static equilibrium (Winter 1986). Rational expectations reduce economics to a stochastic version of perfect foresight (Arrow 1986). Despite his enormous influence on economic policy, Lucas clearly did not intend to contribute to a theory for the *economy we live in* but instead to an artificial world.

---

[2]   W. Samuelson and Zeckhauser (1988) found that status quo bias creates strong ties between beer drinkers and "their" brand.

In Keynes' theory, expectations suffer from uncertainty and differ radically from rational expectations, which became popular in the neoclassical counterrevolution. Expectations are the basis for Keynes' theory's endogenous economic instability because they affect today's demand. Therefore, "[...] a mere change in expectation is capable of producing an oscillation of the same kind of shape as a cyclical movement, in the course of working itself out" (Keynes 1936: 49). In Keynes' theory, historical time is a central element that cannot be reduced to an analytical category or even ignored. Keynes' *General Theory* assumed existing skills, technology, and equipment, not taking into account changes in these variables. This allowed him to apply static methodology. Tobin (1975) called this an inconsistency in Keynes' theory because "his model produces a solution in which, in general, the stock of capital, and other stocks are not constant. Changes in these stocks will in turn alter investment, saving, and other behavior" (195).[3] There is always a time lag between the decision to produce (and invest) and final demand (investment, consumption). Furthermore, effective demand based on expectations requires historical analysis with historical time in the investigation. History affects aspirations and changes preferences. The entrepreneur has to form the best expectations upon which business decisions depend.

5.2   SHORT-TERM, LONG-TERM EXPECTATIONS

There can be a substantial delay between the time that production costs are incurred and the final demand.

> Meanwhile the entrepreneur (including both the producer and the investor in this description)[4] has to form the best expectations he can as to what the consumers will be prepared to pay when he is ready to supply them (directly or indirectly) after the elapse of what may be a lengthy period; and he has no choice but to be guided by these expectations, if he is to produce at all by processes which occupy time. (Keynes 1936: 46)

Therefore, according to Keynes, business decisions fall into two groups:

---

[3]   The Harrod-Domar model (Harrod 1939; Domar 1946) analyzes the interaction of demand and supply on path of economic growth.

[4]   Keynes distinguishes producers who usually have a longer time horizon from investors who may simply speculate and have a short time horizon.

Type 1 (short-term expectations): "[…] the price which a manufacturer can expect to get for his 'finished' output at the time when he commits himself to starting the process which will produce it […]" (Keynes 1936: 46).

Type 2 (long-term expectations): "[…] what the entrepreneur can hope to earn in the shape of future returns if he purchases (or, perhaps, manufactures) 'finished' output as an addition to his capital equipment" (Keynes 1936: 47).

Decisions based on short-term expectations are frequent enough to be classified as routines. Although sales expectations in the next period are affected by uncertainty, the confidence in the entrepreneur's expectations is higher than in the medium or long term, especially when significant investments are necessary. For long-term decisions, reasoning will be more elaborate, increasing the confidence in the expected trends, but uncertainty will remain due to the precariousness of knowledge.

> If we speak frankly, we have to admit that our basis of knowledge for esti-mating the yield ten years hence of a railway, a copper mine, a textile factory, the goodwill of a patent medicine, an Atlantic liner, a building in the City of London amounts to little and sometimes to nothing; or even five years hence. (Keynes 1936: 149–150)

The firms' employment decisions depend on management's expecta-tions: "The actually realised results of the production and sale of output will only be relevant to employment in so far as they cause a modification of subsequent expectations" (Keynes 1936: 47). But under uncertainty, the basis for expectation cannot be rational—based on calculations—but rather depends on confidence. "It is reasonable, therefore, to be guided to a considerable degree by the facts about which we feel somewhat confi-dent, even though they may be less decisively relevant to the issue than other facts about which our knowledge is vague and scanty" (Keynes 1936: 148). This citation refers to availability and representativeness, heuristics that use similar facts that are readily available or representative (Kahneman 2002). Or it may replace more complex circumstances with simpler ones (Kahneman 2011).

> The state of long-term expectation, upon which our decisions are based, does not solely depend, therefore, on the most probable forecast we can make. It also depends on the *confidence* with which we make this forecast—on how highly we rate the likelihood of our best forecast turning out quite wrong. (Keynes 1936: 148, emphasis in original)

A heuristic is a simple procedure that helps find satisfactory albeit imperfect and probably biased answers to complex questions (Kahneman 2011). However, heuristics are a fast but possibly suboptimal method for decisions. Gigerenzer's gaze heuristics applied, for example, in ball games is a prime example: Using gaze heuristics in tennis is not a substitute for the calculations of the speed, spin, and direction but focusing the ball is the optimal solution for the return. One may argue that relying on heuristics is super-rational—optimizing—if the decision costs are considered. Heuristics save search costs, calculations, and decision costs—similar to Mankiw's (1985) menu costs in New Keynesian economics. However, to claim that heuristics are super-rational requires even more complex evaluations than "ordinary" optimization.

> For this reason the facts of the existing situation enter, in a sense disproportionally, into the formation of our long-term expectations; our usual practice being to take the existing situation and to project it into the future, modified only to the extent that we have more or less definite reasons for expecting a change. (Keynes 1936: 148)

What Keynes describes is the status quo bias, the option "to do nothing," to continue in the routines which is a widely observed behavior seen in the selection of pension and health plans, journal subscriptions, in business and private life. "Faced with new options, decision makers often stick with the status quo alternative, for example, to follow customary company policy, to elect an incumbent to still another term in office, to purchase the same product brands, or to stay in the same job" (W. Samuelson & Zeckhauser 1988: 8).

In several experiments, W. Samuelson and Zeckhauser found that the status quo bias becomes stronger with the number of options. However, status quo bias is not a mistake but most subjects being briefed over the experiments' results were surprised that they had this bias. Nevertheless, it was difficult to convince the decision-makers to give all options equal weight. However, in experiments, the status quo bias may be more relevant than in *the world we live in* because actual decisions may initiate more efforts. "In practice we have tacitly agreed, as a rule, to fall back on what is, in truth, a convention" (Keynes 1936: 152). The precarious knowledge basis of future trends arises from mass psychology's sudden fluctuations in public opinion. The formation and the bursting of bubbles can occur in all markets, not only in financial markets (Aliber & Kindleberger 2015; Kindleberger 1978). Keynes emphasizes that professional consultants focus on information advantages to keep ahead of the public. Professional investors and speculators are concerned with the short-term valuation of investments, not the long-term evaluation of investments.[5]

5.3   EXPECTATIONS AND EXPERIENCE

Many findings of Behavioral Economics suggest that the assumption of stable preferences and unbiased perception underlying the neoclassical model do not hold. To maximize utility experienced in the future requires correct knowledge of a specific product or action in the future. But expected utility today might deviate substantially from utility experienced in the future. A necessary condition for utility-maximizing choices is accurate and unbiased forecasts of the hedonic outcomes of potential decisions (Kahneman & Thaler 2006). In other words, the utility derived from today's decisions in the future must be known, and, of course, the evaluation or the preferences should not change after realization. Preferences, therefore, need to be stable and independent of past decisions. But humans' (expected) utility seems to be determined by their situation, mood, environment, and time. "However, people do not always know what they *will* like, and they are likely to err most severely when the temporal gap is long and when the agent's state and circumstances vary between *t1 and t0*" (Kahneman & Thaler 2006: 223, emphasis in original). The difference between expected and experienced utility may be more severe the more extended the experience lies in the future. For example, the expected utility from the Californian sunshine may differ substantially from the experienced utility after moving. Economic agents must not only rank all possible choices, but they must also discount the future utility into present values, meaning that the measurement of utility needs to be cardinal.

Everybody has been initially happy with a product and then frustrated when it does not meet expectations. Many people sign long-term contracts with fitness clubs hoping to get in shape, only to lose interest in working out a few weeks later. Furthermore, perception is not unbiased

---

[5]   Keynes distinguishes speculation relying on the psychology of the market and from an enterprise relying on forecasting the prospective yield of assets over their whole life (Keynes 1936: 158).

but actively disturbed by disinformation, as exemplified in Akerlof and Shiller's (2015) *phishing for phools*.

5.4 IGNORING TIME: THE RATIONAL EXPECTATIONS REVOLUTION ON SHAKY GROUNDS

The Rational Expectation Hypothesis (REH, Muth 1961) is a modified version of the "perfect market model" in economics. It was the basis of the neoclassical counterrevolution in the 1970s and 1980s when stagflation seemed to suggest the ineffectiveness of expansionary economic policy (see Chapter 7). Rational expectations are an effort to circumvent uncertainty by pressing economic trends into the neoclassical model's static (or steady-state) equilibrium. It is a concept to ignore historical time and "makes the future predictable"; it is "a stochastic version of perfect foresight" (Arrow 1986). Muth (1961) defined "rational expectations" as informed predictions of future events: "I should like to suggest that expectations since they are informed predictions of future events, are essentially the same as the predictions of the relevant economic theory" (316).[6]

Lucas, building on Muth's work, declared the neoclassical model as the relevant economic theory arguing that economic agents form "rational expectations" based on that theory. This made macroeconomic policy endogenous in a very specific way by beginning the analysis with the assumption that the economy is already in the optimal equilibrium where every economic agent achieved their optimal utility, profit-maximizing position. Thus, macroeconomic stimulation only disturbs the market optimum in the short term. Economic agents respond to macroeconomic impulses when first confronted with that policy, but they learn that the economy will return to its initial optimal equilibrium. Economic agents made a mistake because imperfect information led them to misperceive monetary values as real (the veil of money), and therefore they responded to expansionary policy. But Lucas (1986) argued that "rational individuals" do not make systematic mistakes because they learn from them.

---

[6] Kromphardt (1985) emphasizes that the rational expectations hypothesis has been reduced to perfect foresight, meaning that in the aggregate the expected price is an unbiased predictor of the actual price. Other versions would claim the best use of available information or predictions based on the relevant economic theory which could also be Keynesian.

Learning, however, is simply a metaphor for discovering[7] Lucas' model without investigating the learning process. Lucas' "rational expectations" are an effort to bring the determined future into the present (Schettkat 2010). Identifying deviations of predicted from actual values requires a reference. There are two causes of incorrect predictions: the model is not the true model, and/or the parameters applied in the model are not the true parameters. One may assume that the true model and the true parameters are known, but more realistically, both are unknown. Economists have endlessly debated theories and econometric estimations; how can the general public perform these tasks much better? What is the reference? How do individuals know what the right model of the economy is? How do they judge whether deviations are systematic? B. Friedman (1984) used the Volcker disinflation as a natural experiment. Volcker's restrictive monetary policy was announced in advance, and economic agents were well informed about these measures, so according to "rational expectations," they should have adjusted their expectations and behavior. Volcker's disinflation should have occurred without disturbing the real economy (production and employment). Instead, unemployment soared (B. Friedman 1984).

What happens if the economy has shifted away from the initial and presumably optimal equilibrium? In textbooks, comparative static analysis dominates, starting the analysis from the optimal equilibrium; it is usually argued that a shift in the aggregate demand function initiated by fiscal and/or monetary policy leads to substantial but short-lived quantity effect with a modest price rise. But over time, prices rise (i.e., the supply function shifts up), diminishing the quantity effect until only the price effect remains. The economy is back at former quantities but at a higher price level (e.g., Blanchard 2000, Abel, Bernanke and Croushore 2010; Mishkin 2010). This is basically the Lucas narrative which is problematic on at least two grounds: it assumes that the economy is initially in the optimal equilibrium and that the supply capacity is unaffected by the demand expansion. However, if additional demand is mainly in investment, the productive capacity will surely rise. Therefore, it may be

---

[7]   Learning may be defined as opening a new territory, things and methods which do not exist before as Arrow's learning by doing where new investments for example lead to innovations in other areas. For Lucas, learning is the discovery of existing relations as a natural law.

misleading to treat the economy as a predetermined system ignoring the options.

Why should there be inflation in response to an expansionary macroeconomic policy if the economy is not at full capacity (full employment)? What happens to workers erroneously pulled into employment? Will higher prices eat up their wage rises? Will all income components (earned and unearned income) be affected similarly? Schettkat and Jovicic (2017) analyzed the Lucas and Sargent narrative, strictly applying neoclassical microfoundations but identifying steps in the alleged process and establishing at least four significant inconsistencies.[8] First, if employers hire workers in response to a macroeconomic impulse, misperceived or not, they will increase production. Second, the neoclassical model to attract workers requires higher (real) wages. How can that go unnoticed by management? Third, firms are embedded in production chains. In other words, they will notice rising prices of intermediate products. Fourth, firms indeed register variations in demand, not only in prices. In any case, learning requires time; workers need time to discover that they had been misled by nominal variables and mistakenly accepted jobs that drove them away from their utility-maximizing position. Employers need to learn that they had mistakenly hired additional workers and probably made the wrong investments. But what is occurring while additional workers are in employment? Is the economy unchanged, or could their production lead to a new equilibrium?

How and why do prices rise if employers—on average, as Lucas and Sargent (1978) mentioned in their paper—do not raise them but simply observe them? How come prices are rising if nobody raises them (Arrow 1959)? Are customers raising the price? Assuming that the price is determined in atomistic, fully competitive markets, a higher price results from the intersection of the unchanged supply function with an upward shifted demand function representing higher quantities, but that was going unnoticed? However, if firms misinterpreted a general price rise as specific for their products (money illusion) and the supply function had not changed, demand must have increased for prices to rise—even in a static setting. Lucas and Sargent only analyze the economy from the supply side and assume that prices come from nowhere. If prices rise first, who is increasing demand? Firms are usually integrated into a production chain

---

[8]   Inflationary effects will raise labor supply of those individuals which rely on transfers because of the resulting negative (real) income effect.

(meaning that they buy intermediate products), observing rising prices. Workers not only provide labor, but they also are consumers. Is the rise in prices going unnoticed?

5.5   SEQUENTIAL VS. TIMELESS PROCESSES: DO MARKETS SELECT THE BEST?

Smith (1776) famously explained the advantages of specialization with his pin-needle example. Specialization in the manufacturing of pin-needles, Smith argued, raises productivity that is only limited by the size of the market. The larger the market, the more specialization it allows. The transportation infrastructure, like the railroads in the United States (Fishlow 1965), extended the markets and enabled productivity to grow through economies of scale. The economics of the EU's Common Market was also based on the productivity effects of an enlarged market without tariffs and non-tariff barriers. Young (1928)[9] argued that the size of the market depends not only on geography but also on productivity: rising productivity raises income, leading to a higher demand that allows for further specialization, a self-enforcing mechanism, and positive feedback. In microeconomic textbooks, the falling part of the cost function is usually defined as economically irrelevant because it is advantageous to expand production to the point where marginal costs increase, and economic analysis often starts. Continuously falling marginal prices are declared to be a seldom occurring monopoly phenomenon.[10] Monopsonies on the demand side, appearing in labor markets, are even less discussed (see for a discussion Card & Krueger 1995, Manning 2003, Stigler 1946). At the firm level, economies of scale cause falling production costs and allow for declining prices. In other words, among

---

[9]   Keynes did not refer to Young's *Economic Journal* paper (1928) on increasing returns in the *General Theory* although he was the editor of that journal. In his response to Dunlop and Tarshis, Keynes (1939) argued that declining marginal costs are favoring his proposal for an expansionary policy.

[10]   Price-setting according to marginal costs will result in deficits until average costs are lower than the marginal costs. Although the standard assumption, pricing to marginal costs, seems not to be the dominant pricing strategy (see Blinder et al. 1998). For today's manufacturing products with high initial developments costs (cars, airplanes, computers, software) declining marginal costs seems common (Kaldor 1972; Salter 1960, Appelbaum & Schettkat 1995).

otherwise identical firms, the one that captures a higher market share will enhance its advantage: a "winner takes all market" (Arthur 1994b).

Kaldor (1972), referring Young, emphasized the importance of the economies of scale, arguing that the equilibrium concept of the neo-classical model is misleading. Indeed, positive feedback effects cause non-ergodic processes. In other words, the sequence of events affects the long-run outcome. Non-ergodic processes occur, for example, in the adaption and development of technologies which usually improve with the number of applications, as Arthur (1994a) nicely demonstrated (see also below). Bernoulli's Petersburg game, which led to the widely used Expected Utility Theory, is non-ergodic. However, it is interpreted as ergodic, leading to wrong conclusions (Peters & Gell-Mann 2016).

The choice of a technology that develops with the number of applications suffers from extreme uncertainty because the future development path is endogenous and unknown. What seems to be the most efficient technology today may not be the best choice in the long run. Switching to another technology may be very costly (inflexibility occurs if significant infrastructure investments are necessary, like switching from combustion to electrical engines) or even impossible if alternatives did not develop. The use of the combustion engines against electrical motors for cars may be illustrative. Although initially without a clear advantage, the former increased its efficiency with the number of applications and dominated the market until very recently, when the environmental costs became visible. It is not impossible to switch to electric cars, but it is enormously costly. How then to choose the right technology if the development path is uncertain? Suppose one is confident that a particular technology will be most efficient in the long run. In that case, one may need subsidies to convince buyers to purchase the less efficient (more expensive) technology. Of course, such a strategy has to concentrate on a few technologies. Although improvements can be expected, the extent remains uncertain.

The often-made argument that the market rather than bureaucrats should choose the technology is misleading in case of increasing returns because market participants are supposed to select the best technology today. They also cannot predict the market development, nor would it be relevant to their present decision. To illustrate the point, suppose that two technologies serve the same purpose but that their efficiency develops differently with the number of applications (over time). There is a funda-mental difference in path dependence depending on whether the returns (the usefulness) decline with every application (decreasing returns) or whether they rise (increasing returns). Suppose that buyers have no preference for a specific technology but choose the one with the higher returns (the less expensive) as the only criterion. With decreasing returns to applications (left diagram in Figure 5.1), the first buyer in the market will choose technology A, as will the subsequent buyers until A's returns have fallen to the starting level of technology B (i.e., until X applications). From that point on, buyers will shift between the two technologies which coexist in the market; the process is flexible and path-efficient. The more efficient technology is used independently from the starting point and the applications in the long run. However, it is challenging to find technologies with decreasing returns to applications; the general case is that technology improves with the number of applications.[11]

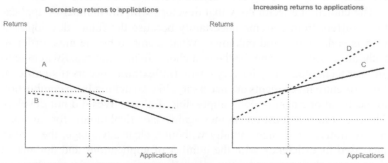

Note: With decreasing returns to applications (left diagram) both technologies will remain in the market, the market process is ergodic. With increasing returns to application (right diagram) technology C will dominate the market because of its initially higher returns which improve over time, enhancing C's advantage over D. D's returns remain at its initial returns; the process is non-ergodic.
Source: Inspired by Arthur (1994a).

Figure 5.1   *Sequential choice of technology with increasing and*
               decreasing returns

Now, assume that the technologies improve with the number of applications so that each application provides higher returns than the preceding

---

[11]   Decreasing returns to the number of applications would occur with "social goods" which are valued by their uniqueness (see Hirsch 1976). Network effects may cause the less efficient technology to survive as illustrated with QWERTY, the keyboard design developed to slow typing on mechanical typewriters but the same design is still used for computer keyboards (David 1990).

ones (right diagram in Figure 5.1). Early buyers will choose technology C, as will all subsequent buyers, because C improves with its applications. The market will never switch to technology D because the returns of D remain at the initial level since nobody bought D. C is the "winner takes all," but C would be inefficient in the long run. If D had the chance to develop, it would offer higher returns. After Y applications, the returns of D would be higher than that of C, but since nobody bought D, the technology did not develop, its returns are stuck at the initial level. The sequence of applications—or buys—affects the outcome, the process is non-ergodic, and one may get stuck in a less efficient technology; it may be not impossible to switch but very costly; the process is inflexible. The development path may be inefficient as opposed to the process presented in the left diagram of Figure 5.1, where the sequences are unimportant in the long run, meaning that it is an ergodic process.

The assumption that markets achieve equilibrium quickly (in the neo-classical model interpreted as the optimum) is explicit or implicit apparent in large parts of economics and in the methods applied to estimate potential production capacity (or the natural rate of unemployment, see Chapter 7). For example, an economy's potential (i.e., production capacity) is often estimated and forecasted by its trend taken as the equilibrium development path.[12] The economy is assumed to be in or return quickly to equilibrium. Since markets are supposed to be endogenously stable, external shocks may push the economy out of this equilibrium. Since small shocks result in small and short-lived disturbances, a bell curve represents "stochastic harmony."

5.6 BERNOULLI'S ERROR II: ENSEMBLE VS. TEMPORAL

Rational decisions rely on expected value (expected utility) calculated by multiplying probability with payoffs (utility) which is the generally accepted method since Bernoulli's (1738) work on the Petersburg Paradox. However, Peters and Gell-Mann (2016) emphasize that this procedure relies on ergodic processes in which time and the sequence of events are irrelevant. Peters and Gell-Mann ascribed the discovery

---

[12]   In the simplest form a linear trend is used but also other methods known as filtering rely on the same principal assumptions of equilibrium. For a deviating approach using the maxima to determine the potential, see Okun (1981).

of non-ergodic processes to Boltzmann and applied it to calculate the expected value of the succession of independent events. In ergodic processes, the ensemble average and the time average converge, but in non-ergodic processes, they do not. The sequence of events is of utmost importance for the individual gambler because she either loses or wins.

To illustrate the difference, if the same (ideal) dice is tossed 10,000 times, we expect the average of the numbers shown to be around 3.5 (the expected value). Similarly, if 10,000 different (ideal) dice are each tossed once, we expect the average of the numbers shown to converge to 3.5. The expected value does not depend on whether the same dice is thrown 10,000 times or whether 10,000 different dice are each tossed once. The outcome is independent when the high numbers occur, whether they are concentrated in a certain period or are evenly distributed over the period. Timing does not matter; the sequence of outcomes can be ignored; the time average assembles the ensemble average; it is an ergodic process. This is different if the individual wealth after a sequence of draws is considered if wealth in the second draw depends on the results of the first draw and develops over time as in Bernoulli's Petersburg game or as in the variation of the game Peters (2019) constructed. These games are non-ergodic, meaning that the sequence of events matters.

Peters (2019) impressively illustrates the payoff in a non-ergodic gamble with a variation of Bernoulli's game but with an unfair mathematical structure in favor of the player (with a positive expected value). The change in wealth (Δx) in Peters' game is 0.5 of x (the current wealth) with a probability of ½ and -0.4 of x with a probability of ½ (thus the expected value is ½ $(0.5 - 0.4)$ x = 0.05x) resulting in an exponential function of expected wealth (x) with the number of draws (the linear straight function in Figure 5.2).[13] But this upward-sloping function represents the ensemble average (which results in losses for the organizer of the game); it is cumulative wealth from the expected values of single draws, which are 0.05x in every round. This value is interesting for the organizer of the game, who in this specific game[14] can expect to lose "in the long run," so after many draws, but the individual gambler either wins (0.5x) or loses (-0.4x) in a draw. The cumulated wealth an individual

¹³   In Bernoulli's game the loss of accumulated wealth was 100% when losing although the game was presented without an upfront participating fee.

¹⁴   Casinos and insurances, of course, bias the probabilities for their advantage. The specific game illustrates that even in games mathematically unfair in favor of the gambler, they cannot account on the expected value of the ensemble.

gambler can expect is different because they cannot rely on the ensemble average but rather on the time average. Peters provides simulations of 150 individual paths showing that the time average (of his mathematically unfair game favoring the gambler!) is negative for the gambler. Although some gamblers may be lucky for a short while (the points in the cloud above the horizontal), most single gambles result in a deficit.

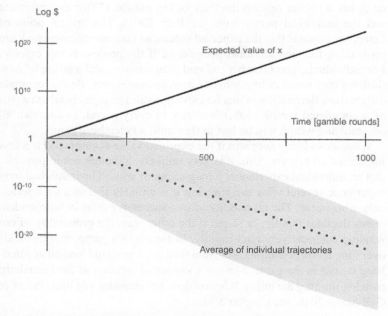

Note: The straight line shows the expected value of x in log $ as a function of time (rounds of the gamble). The x function increases because the average wins ½ *0.5x and losses ½*-0.4 equals the expected gain of 0.1x each round (the assemble mean). This is a game predicting a loss for the organizer after many repeated rounds (law of big numbers). The dotted line shows the average of 150 simulated individual trajectories with 1000 rounds each.
Source: Data were taken from Peters (2019: Fig 2), approximate illustration.

Figure 5.2   *Peters' diagram stylized (randomly generated trajectories of Peters' example)*

Why the difference? The expected value of a single draw is the average of the win and the loss (½ (0.5 – 0.4) x = 0.05x), so wins and losses are compensated. The ensemble outcome results from the single draw times the number of repetitions, the upward sloping function of expected values in Figure 5.2. However, individual wealth depends on the sequence of events. Suppose the first draw wins, the wealth of the gambler increases by 50%, which is not—as in the ensemble—compensated by a loss. The procedure is similar to insurance: For the individual, the accident happens or not, the expected value of the ensemble is relevant for the insurance company who can rely on the "law of big numbers" (for the insurance and the individual perspective, see Barr 2001). The critical point of Peters' example is that the expected values, as commonly calculated, are misleading for the individual perspective if the process is not ergodic. For individuals, one false bet can end their gamble, and a string of misfortunes may result in heavy losses or even bankruptcy. Peters' example differs from Bernoulli's in that he looks at wealth changes in which a part of accumulated wealth (40%) is at risk in every round. In contrast, all accumulated wealth will be lost in Bernoulli's Petersburg game.

What looks like a sure win if the expected value is computed is a loss for almost all players. Still, it is very unlikely, although not impossible, that an individual experiences a long string of wins. The individual may experience several wins in a row, but it is unlikely that in a time series, only wins occur. The probability of two successive wins in independent tosses declines rapidly, or to put it the other way, the probability of not winning consecutively rises rapidly. In Bernoulli's game, wealth builds over time if one is winning, but from then on, one would lose all accumulated wealth in the game. Menger's suggested solution to the Petersburg paradox limiting the utility function does not consider this loss (Peters & Gell-Mann 2016, see Chapter 3.1).

5.7   DISCOUNT RATES AFFECTED BY MAGNITUDES

Suppose that economic agents make *rational choices* and maximize their own utility, which requires knowledge of a specific product's or action's future utility. In other words, today's expected utility must fit the utility experienced in the future. In addition, to decide between alternatives, a probability must be assigned to each specific outcome. That being said, expected and experienced utility may differ for various reasons: utility may change when a person owns the product (that is that the endowment effect or habituation changes the preferences), the knowledge of the utility before actually holding the product is limited, current moods influence expected utility, expectations may be biased.

Economists project the future into the present by applying discounting. When evaluating an investment, for example, the expected gains in the future are discounted at a specific rate. In contrast, the compound interest method projects the present into the future, answering the question of what a particular amount put into an account today would be worth in the future. Of course, the values depend on the interest rate. Discounting is the standard procedure to evaluate investments in business economics. If the discounted expected future gains are higher than the costs of the investment, it is expected to be profitable. It is also of enormous relevance when evaluating investments preventing future damage, as with climate change. How much should we invest today to prevent future damage? If the discounted value of expected damage (costs) is higher than the investment preventing this damage in absolute terms, the investments are profitable. Obviously, the discount rate affects the decision. Should the private discount rate (the bank interest rate) or a lower social discount rate be applied? When evaluating the living conditions of future generations, many prominent economists argue that a discount rate of zero is appropriate because the utility of following generations should be valued the same as the utility of the current population.

The *Stern Review* (Stern 2006) presented estimates of future damage caused by carbon emissions. It was especially criticized for using a low discount rate, resulting in high present values of future damages and thus justifying comparatively high preventive investments. In other words, the discount rate affects the distribution of burdens over the generations. In his 1973 Ely Lecture to the American Economic Association on the economics of exhaustible resources, Solow (1974) emphasized that the private discount rate includes individual risks that are irrelevant for society as a whole and that social discount rates should be lower. Stern (2006) wrote: "Future generations should have a right to a standard of living no lower than the current one" (Stern 2006: 42). This ethical position requires a low discount rate (even a zero rate) shared by many well-known economists, including Ramsey, Harrod, Solow, and Arrow (Stern 2006: 48).

Keynes (1930) was not concerned with global environmental damage but was quite optimistic about the general development of wealth, overcoming scarcity as exemplified in his "the economic possibilities for our grandchildren,"[15] but he argued in favor of high discount rates. "[...] life is not long enough; human nature desires quick results, there is a peculiar zest in making money quickly, and remoter gains are discounted by the average man at a very high rate" (Keynes 1936: 157). This statement requires constant or even rising discount rates with time, but this is not what Behavioral Economics finds. A summary of 42 empirical studies on discount rates (Wilkinson 2008: 314–317) found that discount rates do not rise with time as diminishing marginal utility with time would suggest, but that they instead decline. Humans do not seem to apply exponential discounting (discounting at a constant or rising discount rate) but instead, use hyperbolic discounting (Ainslie 1991). In addition, an established result in Behavioral Economics is that higher amounts are discounted at lower rates than smaller amounts (Kahneman & Tversky 2000). Magnitudes influence the same person's discount rates but in the reverse order of the *rational choice* assumption: the higher the amounts, the lower the discount rate (Thaler 1981). Forward-looking *rational choice* requires discount rates to increase with time. Income, payments, utility farther in the future should be discounted at higher rates than in the less remote utility (i.e., the discounting function should be exponential). Discounting utility requires a cardinal measurement of utility and assumes that future utility is independent of current choices. In other words, preferences in the future are independent of choices made today because there is no path dependence, no habit formation, and reference points.

Time distance and diminishing marginal utility require the higher values to be discounted at higher rates. Wilkinson found the reverse to be true (Wilkinson 2008). Summarizing empirical discount rates from 42 studies, Wilkinson stated: "It should be noted that the effect works in the opposite direction to the effect of diminishing marginal utility" (Wilkinson 2008: 207). Magnitudes also matter. The evaluation of a future payment seems to be affected by magnitudes. However, "rational discounting" requires discount rates to be independent of the magni-

---

[15]   Keynes' long-run expectations were very optimistic assuming that working hours decline substantially because the expansions of needs was predicted to lag productivity growth. Hagemann (2019) discusses these issues with reference to the thinking of Keynes' contemporaries. Working hours shortened but much less than Keynes predicted (Freeman 2008). The enormous expansion of new additional goods, soon regarded as "necessities" (see Chapter 6.3), prevents the often predicted general saturation (see Kurz 2018).

tude to ensure consistent results. Yet, a common finding in Behavioral Economics is that more significant amounts are discounted at lower rates than smaller amounts (Kahneman & Tversky 2000); the reverse of the rationality assumptions.

Thaler (1981) found that the same people were indifferent to the following choices (Table 5.1):

Table 5.1   Implied discount rates

Immediately	In one year	Implied discount rate
15 [$]	60 [$]	139%
250 [$]	350 [$]	34%
3000 [$]	4000 [$]	29%

Source: Thaler (1981).

The implied discount rates illustrate an amazing variation, depending on the magnitudes, but in the reverse order, as expected under the *rational choice* assumption. The higher the amounts, the lower the discount rate; this is the "money illusion" or simply "irrational." However, it seems a regular pattern.

The order in which choices are presented should not influence a rational individual. Nevertheless, the ordering of options strongly affects human decisions; this is the basis for "nudge" (Thaler & Sunstein 2008). Framing probabilities as gains or losses also influences decisions. Humans seem to discount gains more heavily than losses (prospect theory). Participants in financial markets, closest to the perfect market model (Schettkat 2010), illustrate this behavior; investors tend to keep shares whose prices are falling.

5.8   INTERTEMPORAL MAXIMIZATION

Intertemporal maximization has been advocated to explain labor supply variations over time.[16] It is argued that workers optimize labor supply over time (possibly the lifespan), raising supply (entering the labor market) when wages are high and reducing supply (withdrawing from the labor market) at less favorable conditions (intertemporal substitu-

---

[16]   This issue is often discussed in the lifecycle context, but here the maximization v. habitual behavior is relevant.

tion, voluntary unemployment). Again, this behavior requires stable preferences and a consistent evaluation of current and future incomes, as well as the derived utility. If inflation occurs—even if it is known and understood—future income needs to be corrected, assuming that real income is relevant for utility. However, it is not just the *money illusion*. The experimental evidence suggests that nominal values are also crucial for utility (i.e., happiness).

"Rosie the Riveter," the American factory worker performing even physically demanding hard work during World War II, was—according to the neoclassical labor supply model—attracted into employment by comparatively high wages in the tight labor market but will withdraw once wages normalize when she prefers leisure (nonemployment, unemployment). Rosie maximizes her utility over time by moving in and out of employment according to the wage rates since preferences do not change by assumption. Intertemporal utility maximization is a variant of the hypothesis that variations in employment and unemployment result from the choice between work and leisure. At least since the great depression—after the publication of the *General Theory*—this hypothesis was discarded but revived in natural rate theory (see Chapter 7). Clark and Summers (1982) used historical data to investigate whether the hypothesis of intertemporal utility maximization is consistent with actual labor supply behavior or whether it is habitual because Rosie's work experience changed her lifestyle and preferences. Clark and Summers found that Rosie's cohorts showed significantly higher participation rates even after the normalization of labor market conditions after World War II.[17]

---

[17]   Intertemporal labor supply substitution requires a high elasticity of substitution to achieve realistic results (Martinez, Saez & Siegenthaler 2018).

6.   Socially embedded individuals

6.1   BEHAVIORAL ECONOMICS CONFIRMING KEYNES' OBSERVATIONS OF WAGE BEHAVIOR

Just on the first pages of the *General Theory,* Keynes rejected "utility maximization," arguing that the second postulate of the (neo-) classical theory, that the real wage equals the marginal disutility of employment, is a false assumption. Keynes rejected the maximization postulate on empirical grounds: "Whilst workers will usually resist a reduction of money-wages, it is not their practice to withdraw their labour whenever there is a rise in the price of wage-goods" (Keynes 1936: 9). Keynes added: "Wide variations are experienced in the volume of employment without any apparent change either in the minimum real demands of labour or in its productivity" (Keynes 1936: 9).[1]

For (neo-) classical economists, who are accustomed to thinking about models of socially isolated individuals having formed their utility functions independently and who are solely stimulated by real wages, the nominal wage orientation was simply "irrational." And since *homo oeconomicus* is presumably rational, meaning maximizing real variables and interpreting the world without bias, they turned nominal wage resistance into a *money illusion*. This is because, in this theory, money is just a curtain covering the real values. "But, whether logical or illogical, experience shows that this is how labour in fact behaves" (Keynes 1936: 9). This quote underscores Keynes' requirement that economic theory needs to be based on, or at least not in contradiction to, *the world we live in.*

---

[1]   Here, Keynes seem to contradict his acceptance of the first postulate of neoclassical economics, that the real wage equals to the marginal product of labor. In that case, changing employment should result in variations in the marginal product of labor. However, in his response to Dunlop and Tarshis (Keynes 1939) he seems to be prepared to doubt the validity of the first postulate.

The *money illusion* interpretation of Keynes' argument for nominal wage resistance is totally ignorant to the reasoning Keynes was clearly stating that the individual's or the microunit's position in society matters.

> ... any individual or group of individuals, who consent to a reduction of money-wages relatively to others, will suffer a *relative* reduction in real wages, which is a sufficient justification for them to resist it. On the other hand, it would be impracticable to resist every reduction of real wages, due to a change in the purchasing-power of money which affects all workers .... (Keynes 1936: 14)

Solow (1979: 79) argues: "[…] in a decentralized labor market, every change in a nominal wage is also a change in relative wages; workers can and do resist reductions in their relative wages in the only way the institutions allow […]," which seems to be in line with Keynes. Theory, in line with actual observed human behavior, with empirical facts, was Keynes' ambition: Solow adds that one may be easily convinced that workers resist nominal wage reductions, but the difficult question becomes, why employers do not take advantage of recessions (excess labor supply) and lower the wages of their workforce or substitute their workforce with unemployed workers at lower wages.

The *money illusion* interpretation of nominal wage resistance is an example of theory working as blinders. The neoclassical model assumes the isolation of the individual from society. Their utility functions are assumed to be independent of each other. They care solely about their own well-being, depending only on the goods and services they consume (real income) and their leisure time. Assuming well-shaped (convex) and stable preference curves, the individual chooses the income–leisure combination which maximizes the individual's utility, depending on the real wage. This equals the marginal disutility of work or the marginal utility of consumption. Nominal wages are unimportant; only real wages count.

The interaction of individuals is restricted to the market exchange (e.g., consumption of other individuals may affect relative prices and thus the budget constraint, but the utility functions remain unaffected). Comparisons of income and consumption among individuals: concerns of the relative position in society affecting the utility functions are excluded from the neoclassical theory, by assumption. Positional goods, fashion, *keeping up with the Joneses*, do not affect the utility of *homo oeconomicus*. Every individual maximizes his or her own utility independently.

Keynes' theory does not abstract from socially embedded individuals. On the contrary, individual utility functions are interdependent and social status is important. This is the core of *nominal wage rigidity*. It is also listed among Keynes' subjective motives for consumption (Keynes 1936). However, the utility functions of socially embedded individuals are directly connected, but much more difficult to analyze, let alone to aggregate (for consumption, see section 4.3).

The neoclassical theory works as blinders. It leads to incorrect conclusions and the non-response of nominal wages in slack labor markets. Their inflexibility became, and still is, the main explanation for unemployment repeated in every talk-show on the subject. If prices are fixed, the argument goes, markets cannot clear and the almost universal recipe for battling unemployment is the downward flexibility of wages. However, as Keynes laid out in Chapter 19 of the *General Theory*, downward nominal wage flexibility would make a recession worse and would not result in lower real wages, because it would lower prices if the markets were competitive. What may be an attractive micro policy, a measure for an individual firm, will turn out to be counterproductive at the macro level, especially if the perfect market model is assumed to hold (see Hahn & Solow 1986).[2]

Theory, in line with actual observed human behavior, with empirical facts, was Keynes' ambition. The main findings in Behavioral Economics can be read as strong confirmation of Keynes' observations, representing human behavior in *the world we live in*. Situations are evaluated from a reference point, often the status quo (endowment effect), from which gains and losses have asymmetrical utility effects. Losses reduce utility more than similar gains raise it (prospect theory, loss aversion). Individuals care about fairness and its violation may even outweigh individual gains. Higher money values also improve happiness: Controlling for real values (actually products), subjects showed in functional magnetic resonance brain imaging (fMRI) stronger reactions when higher prices are assigned to identical products (Rangel, Wibral, & Falk 2009). Is that money illusion, a mistake, or is it that money values serve as reference? Anyway, it seems that money values are an important aspect of human behavior.

The importance of nominal values is impressively revealed in a study by Shafir, Diamond and Tversky (1997). Participants were asked to indicate who was better off, in monetary terms and in satisfaction, A or

---

[2]   Wage flexibility is also a two-sided sword of downward and upward wage changes (Bell & Freeman 1985).

Table 6.1   *Preferences nominal and real*

Person	1st year			2nd year		Respondents Thought:		
	Salary	Inflation	End Year Pay Rise	Salary	Real	Better off Economic- ally	Happier	Propensity to Quit
	1	2	3	4	5	6	7	8
A	30,000$	0%	2%	30,600$	30,600$	71%	36%	65%
B	30,000$	4%	5%	31,500$	30,300$	29%	64%	35%

Source: Compilation from Shafir, Diamond and Tversky (1997) cited in Wilkinson (2008: 32/33).

B, graduates of the same college, but facing different pay increases and inflation (Table 6.1).

The participants in the Shafir, Diamond and Tversky (1997) study understood the differences between nominal and real income very well (Column 6). At the end of the year, Person B earns the higher nominal income, but also encounters inflation. Person A is judged to be financially better off, where most respondents do not suffer from the *money illusion.* Nevertheless, most respondents thought that the higher nominal income that Person B receives makes them happier (Column 7). Person A (the person better off in real terms) is more likely to quit their job if they receive a better job offer (Column 8).

This finding sheds light on a conundrum in labor economics, where it was found that upward sloping wage profiles are not necessarily related to increases in productivity (Medoff & Abraham 1980, 1981). In actuality, workers seem to prefer increasing wage profiles, even if the advantage of declining wage profiles (high wages at the beginning of the career) is explained to them (Loewenstein & Sicherman 1991). When Californian teachers were offered a choice to split their annual salary into 10 or into 12 payments, they overwhelmingly chose 12 (i.e., they paid for self-control). Other examples include payments for diets and high-interest credit cards.

Based on the income and job satisfaction data for 5000 workers in Great Britain, Clark and Oswald (1996) conclude that workers care about relative wages. In summary: "These results appear to offer statistical credence to the hypothesis that feelings of well-being depend on a reference or comparison level of income. By contrast, they provide little support for the simple view, presented in microeconomics textbooks, that a worker's level of well-being is a function of absolute income" (Clark & Oswald 1996: 373). Bracha, Gneezy and Loewenstein (2015) find that labor supply responds to relative pay in the assumed direction but accept pay differential for good reasons such as educational differences.

Probably the most compelling evidence for the importance of relative pay results from experiments using magnetic resonance imaging. Brain activity increases with absolute income, but controlled for absolute income, relative income is important (Dohmen et al. 2011, Fliessbach et al. 2007). Reference levels (e.g., minimum wages) even serve as a reference point after they have been removed (Falk, Fehr & Zehnder 2006). Neumark and Postlewaite (1998) tested the law of relative incomes for utility and found that a woman's decision to start paid work depends on whether her sisters and sisters-in-law are employed and how much they earn. Thurow (1975) reported results from Gallup questionnaires asking United States citizens about the minimum amount of money a family of four needs to survive. Over a 17-year period, the answers fell between 53% to 59% of the average income, although average income rose substantially.

Labor supply decisions have long been related to habit formation. Comparing the labor force participation of women during World War II ("Rosie the Riveter") and after that date, Clark and Summers (1982) found that the cohorts of women who were employed during World War II showed higher labor force participation, even after World War II. If women were attracted to employment solely by high wages during World War II, they should have withdrawn from normalized after-war labor markets. However, their participation rates remained higher, which Clark and Summers interpreted as habit formation (i.e., their participation in labor markets has changed their preferences towards work, towards income, towards consumption). In other words, their reference points changed (section 4.4).

6.2   CONSUMPTION

Keynes (1936) describes the effects on consumption as short-term, long-term, objective and subjective. Among the subjective factors, he lists "[...] Enjoyment, Shortsightedness, Generosity, Miscalculation, Ostentation and Extravagance" (108). This list is amazing for neoclassical economists since, again, Keynes recognizes the socially embedded individual. Ostentation certainly cannot be a spending motive for the socially isolated *homo oeconomicus*. Keynes' list could come right out of a "Behavioral Economics" book.

Frank (1985: 146) observes: "To many economists, the notion of consumers being strongly influenced by demonstration effects must have seemed troublingly inconsistent with the reasoned pursuit of self-interest, if not completely irrational." Nevertheless, several economists took relative positions and social interactions into account. *Keeping up with the Joneses*, from Veblen (1899), is an early example. Duesenberry (1949: 48) argued: "Any particular consumer will be more influenced by the consumption of people with whom he has social contacts [...]" In addition, of course, past consumption/income may serve as a reference point, leading to path dependence (or habituation) leading to ratchet effects.

Frank (1999) argued that the consumption of the neighbors, the Joneses, as a reference, were substituted by the consumption of the very wealthy through mass media, which arguably leads to overconsumption. Signaling social status, lifestyle through consumption (in the wider sense) is important for socially embedded individuals (Hirsch 1976, Leibenstein 1976).[3]

> The fundamental psychological law, upon which we are entitled to depend with great confidence both *a priori* from our knowledge of human nature and from the detailed facts of experience, is that men are disposed, as a rule and on the average, to increase their consumption as their income increases, but not by as much as the increase in their income. (Keynes 1936: 96)

This stability in consumption, relative to income, was thought to be characteristic for short periods, for cyclical fluctuations, when there was not enough time to adapt to changed objective circumstances.

> For a man's habitual standard of life usually has the first claim on his income, and he is apt to save the difference which discovers itself between his actual income and the expense of his habitual standard; [...] Thus a rising income will often be accompanied by increased saving, and a falling income by decreased saving, on a greater scale at first than subsequently. (Keynes 1936: 97)

---

[3]   Wisman (2022) argues that if "Keynes had read more Veblen" he would have emphasized social embeddedness of consumption more than he did. However, social embeddedness is central in Keynes labor supply analysis.

This statement of Keynes can be interpreted as a description of Duesenberry's (1949) ratchet effects, caused by habituation, reference points in the modern Behavioral Economics literature.

Reference points depend on experienced consumption and employment patterns (i.e., habituation). They also depend on the observed patterns of the reference groups (Baxter 1988), which itself are affected by the cultural influences, making preferences endogenous (Drakopoulos 2011). Keynes' fundamental psychological law refers to the short-term objective factors. However, in the long term, he recognizes subjective factors:

> The amount that the community spends on consumption obviously depends (i) partly on the amount of its income, (ii) partly on the other objective attendant circumstances, and (iii) partly on the subjective needs and the psychological propensities and habits of the individuals composing it and the principles on which the income is divided between them (which may suffer modification as output is increased). (Keynes 1936: 90–91)

Keynes regards the subjective motives as roughly stable, although they may vary over the long term and between countries or regions. In the short term, he assumes the objective factors (e.g., changes in the wage-unit, changes in fiscal policy) are most relevant, whereas the other factors (e.g., windfall change in capital-values, wealth effect, changes in the rate of time-discounting, changes in the expectations of the relationship between the present and future level of income) are, at most, marginally significant. In the long term, and aside from income, he allows for changes in the propensity to consume.

Keynes argues that changes in the expectations of future incomes are too uncertain to exert much influence (on average, although not necessarily for an individual), which may be read as a pre-publication neglect of Friedman's permanent income hypothesis (Friedman 1957), which relies on the (right) expectations on future incomes.

6.3   THE IMPACT OF ENDOGENOUS PREFERENCES. IF HISTORY MATTERS

The valuation of situations related to a reference point is arguably the most important finding in Behavioral Economics, especially for methodological concerns. The endowment effect (Kahneman, Knetsch & Thaler 1991) refers to changes in the valuation of products, depending on the procession of a product, which then changes the indifference curve.

When buying a product, its utility should be equal to the utility of the money that was paid for it (respectively, to the alternative products the money could have bought). It turns out, however, that once a product is possessed, it would only be sold at a significantly higher price, although the owner would not have paid the potential selling price. The utility for the owner, derived from the possession of the product, must have risen after he/she possessed it. Put another way, preferences are endogenous and are evaluated asymmetrically. Similar effects are described with prospect theory, where adding an additional unit of a certain product raises the utility by less than how the subtraction of a unit of the very same product would reduce the utility. Thus, the orientation on reference points implies changes in the utility function (i.e., the neoclassical assumption of stable preferences is violated).

If humans evaluate gains and losses relative to a reference point (i.e., the status quo), the indifference curves change their shape around the reference point. Given the myriad of choices, utility maximization is already difficult if preference curves are assumed to be stable in a static environment. If preference curves shift or change their shape, if the utility of various choices changes, depending on the decisions made in the past, maximization is much harder, if not impossible, and dynamic optimization would be required (Pesendorfer 2006). Individuals would not only have to evaluate the utility of the myriad of options they are facing. They would also have to evaluate the changes in utility once certain decisions have been made. As Pesendorfer put it:

> In a standard model, maximizing a utility function is simply a concise representation of how the agent behaves. But once the model is interpreted as a mental process, we must imagine that the decision maker actually performs the optimization. Since the decision maker is systematically wrong about future behavior there is no obvious benefit from maximizing the objective function as opposed to taking some other (perhaps arbitrary) action. (2006: 9)

Pesendorfer argues that the reference-point orientation of preferences is not compatible with the basic axioms of neoclassical economics.

One might also argue that rational individuals do not perform the optimization procedure, because they know that once a decision has been made, preferences will change around the reference point. Integrating all the potential changes is just not paying off. A sort of optimization of the decision process, which fits *homo oeconomicus'* rationality but, which, of course, is also the justification for heuristics and other fast decision procedures. Whatever the underlying reasoning, be it the impossibility of the dynamic optimization of the myriad of options or a rational decision not undertaking the efforts, the consequence for actual choices is that non-optimizing decision procedures are applied.

Komlos (2014) analyzed the impact of utility, depending on reference points in the framework of conventional indifference curves. He concludes that even after the initial optimization, where the budget constraint is tangential to an indifference curve, kinks will occur at the reference point if there is a tradeoff between the two commodities. This is because of the differing valuation in the gains and losses, according to prospect theory. Komlos (2014) explains that prospect theory changes the marginal rate of substitution between a good X and another good Y (m = $-dY_i/dX_i$), because the loss in Y weighs higher than the gain in X. That being said, when initially approaching the point, the two were equal. In other words, the slope of the indifference curve changed.

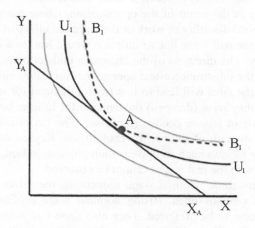

Source: Inspired by Komlos (2014).

Figure 6.1   Behavioral indifference curve

The endowment effect implies that a substitution of X against Y requires *ex post* compared to the initial indifference curves, higher increases in Y to compensate for a loss in X. More specifically, Point A in Figure 6.1 represents the utility maximum, given the budget constraint Y_A-X_A. The utility evaluation of Y and X changes once Point A is achieved. Under loss aversion, the utility loss of X will be higher than the utility gains from Y. In this way, to the left of Point A, the behavioral indifference curve will be steeper (dashed function). To the right of Point A, the behavioral indifference will be flatter. This is because it is compensating for the loss in utility related to a decline in Y, which requires a higher increase in X, when compared to the initial indifference curve $(U_1\text{-}U_1)$. The behavioral indifference curve $(B_1\text{-}B_1)$ will cross the initial preference curve, which violates the assumed well ordered (and stable) preferences and will make the process of optimization even more difficult, if not impossible.

Keynes' labor supply function is a vertical line in the real-wage employment space (the textbook presentation of the labor supply), where the level of labor supply is determined by habits, norms, standard hours, and historical trends. In the nominal-wage employment space, Keynes' labor supply function is horizontal at the current nominal wage, to the left of the current employment, and probably upward sloping, to the right of actual employment. This is in contrast to the neoclassical model, where the labor supply is the result of the optimization, where the real wage equals the marginal disutility of work or the marginal utility of leisure.

A decline in the real wage due to inflation would lead to a change in the labor supply. The direction of the change is undetermined, because the income and the substitution effect operate in reverse directions: lower (higher) real-wage rates will lead to less (more) demand for leisure. At the same time, they raise (dampen) the demand for leisure, because the opportunity costs of leisure decline (increase). The net effect depends on the relative strength of the two reverse effects. Keynes denied that the labor supply follows such an optimization process. Indeed, the labor supply varying with the real wages cannot be observed.

While workers resist nominal wage reductions, the effect of rising nominal wages remains open. Rising nominal wage profiles can be observed and seem to be preferred. They also appear to affect job satisfaction positively. Clark (1999) found evidence for a high significant correlation between job satisfaction and wage increases, but only an insignificant relationship with the current level of income. Freeman (1978) found that job satisfaction reduces, in addition to monetary variables, workers quitting. Labor contracts are stipulated in nominal terms and seem to serve as a reference point. Testing whether the perfect market hypothesis holds that wages are paid according to marginal productivity, Krueger and Summers (1988) regressed individual wages on personal characteristics (e.g., education, experience), job characteristics (occupations) and industries. The latter should be insignificant under the perfect market hypothesis, but it is not.

Industries pay significantly different wages controlled for personal and jobs characteristics. More specifically, standardized workers receive different wages, depending on the industry. The authors interpret their result as a contradiction of the marginal productivity theory of wages and a clear hint that the fair wage hypothesis may hold. According to this hypothesis, firms with high profitability share their rents with their workforce. Therefore, there may be good and bad jobs. Indeed, workers are queuing for higher paying jobs (Thurow 1975, Schettkat 1993), so individual firms may face an upward sloping labor supply function and have at least some discretion in wage-setting (Manning 2003). Collusion, of course, will strengthen their position (Krueger & Ashenfelter 2018). In addition, the number of people that quit their jobs is significantly lower in higher paying industries (Schettkat 1993) and those workers whose pay is unfavorably compared to their colleagues are more likely to search for alternative jobs (Card et al. 2010). This is another reason why firms pay efficiency wages (Schlicht 1978).

Schumpeter (1911), who emphasized the role of product innovations for economic growth, also argued that innovations must be discovered and knowledge of their usefulness must diffuse. The population needs to learn to consume (Witt 2001). Process innovations, the development of new production techniques and reorganization—learning by doing (Arrow 1962)—"democratize" wealth, allowing for declining prices. What was a luxury yesterday may be a necessity today and this process is affected by social relations and moved from comparisons with others to the orientation on the living style of the super–rich enabled by mass media (Frank 1999). All products move through a life cycle characterized by a s-curve: slow diffusion at the start, accelerated diffusion, and saturation (Abernathy & Utterback 1978, Freeman & Soete 1997) when they become a necessity. The PEW Research Center (2006) finds that many goods quickly become necessities; cell phones became within 10 years (1996 to 2006) for 50% Americans a necessity.

A necessary condition for utility-maximizing choices are accurate and unbiased forecasts of the hedonic outcomes of potential choices (Kahneman & Thaler 2006). In other words, the utility derived from a decision in the future must be well known and, of course, the evaluation should not change after realization. Looking from the other side: past decisions should not affect present utility. In other words, preferences need to be stable and independent of past decisions, expected utility must be independent from past choices. However, utility ascribed to a product may differ once a person owns the product (i.e., endowment effect, habituation, change of preferences, path dependence). A widely used example is the choice of a restaurant. Humans seem to value gains less than losses (Bernoulli, prospect theory; Kahneman & Tversky 1979). Participants in financial markets, presumably closest to the perfect market model (Schettkat 2010), illustrate this behavior; investors tend to keep shares although prices are falling.

The findings of Behavioral Economics reveal that humans often make systematic mistakes even in predicting their own future utility. Thus, they fail to maximize their experienced utility. Sometimes humans make the wrong choices because they do not fully understand the situation. But it is not simply error, or the misunderstanding of situations, which results in decisions deviating from *rational choice*. Even when misunderstandings are clarified, "irrational" choices remain. It is not simply the *money illusion,* when nominal values are recognized in decisions, they can even overrule real values with respect to utility.

7. The resurrection and fall of *homo oeconomicus*

7.1   OLD THEORY AHEAD OF THE FACTS?

The discrepancies between Keynesian macroeconomic theory, dominant until the late 1970s and neoclassical microeconomics, were characterized as 'schizophrenia,' two different visions of the economy. Keynes' microeconomic observations led to his macroeconomic conclusions, but they are incompatible with the neoclassical axioms of maximization and optimal equilibrium. These two conflicting visions coexisted in segregation, separated into Keynesian macro and neoclassical micro. Keynes' behavioral observations were widely ignored and declared exceptional cases, whereas the neoclassical axioms—maximization and optimal equilibrium—were stylized as general, the only basis for sound economic theory. How individuals determine their labor supply explains the differences between Keynes' and the neoclassical models. Keynes did not fully develop the underlying labor supply behavior, and labor supply remained mainly within the neoclassical model providing the basis for the neoclassical counterrevolution. Keynes' observation of downward nominal wage rigidity was especially criticized because what matters for *homo oeconomicus'* labor supply are goods, real wages. Change in money wages may only briefly confuse the individuals' labor supply decisions and Phelps (1967, 1968) and Friedman (1968)—with slight variations between the two—attacked Keynesian theory just on the grounds of the neoclassical labor supply model (the second postulate) according to which the marginal disutility of work balances the real wage. Unemployment became again simply the result of utility-maximizing choice, the irritating assumption which contributed to the popularity of Keynes' *General Theory* in the 1930s. The theoretical basis of the neoclassical counterrevolution was the neoclassical labor supply model that failed dramatically in the 1930s.

The downward-sloping Phillips curve—equated with Keynesian economics, the "menu for policy" (Samuelson and Solow 1960)—Phelps, and Friedman argued, is a transitory phenomenon, a short-term deviation from the full employment equilibrium to which the economy will always return. Therefore, the Phillips curve is vertical in the long run, leaving no role for expansionary macroeconomic policies—fiscal or monetary. Assuming the economy is in optimal equilibrium, macroeconomic stimulation will cause inflation but no real effects (no effects on production and employment). The rhetorically brilliant Friedman labeled the unemployment rate compatible with the optimal general equilibrium, the "natural rate of unemployment." Noticing some information imperfections[1] and a certain economic dynamic, Friedman (1968) awkwardly defined the natural rate of unemployment as

> [...] the level of unemployment that would be ground out by the Walrasian system of general equilibrium equations, provided that there is imbedded in them the actual structural characteristics of the labor and commodity markets, including market imperfections, stochastic variability in demands and supplies, the cost of gathering information about job vacancies and labor availabilities, the costs of mobility, and so on. (8)

What a twist: The Walrasian system is a synonym for general equilibrium achieved by instantaneous price reactions keeping the system in equilibrium, abstracting from all distortions. Nevertheless, the published version of Friedman's address to the American Economic Association in 1967 is "[...] very likely the most influential article ever published in an economics journal. Its influence reached way beyond the profession—for example to European and Japanese central banks and to *The Economist* and other opinion leaders" (Tobin 1995: 40).

The natural rate of unemployment became the new full employment (Tobin 1975), purported to depend on real but not monetary factors. "Output is a real magnitude, not a monetary magnitude" (Friedman 2006: 4). Thus, monetary policy is innocent; it does not affect growth and unemployment directly but only indirectly through its effects on expectations. In the words of central bankers: "Other than by maintaining

---

[1]   The use of imperfections indicates the overly strong orientation on an abstract theoretical model which assumes perfect information—complete knowledge—as normal; contrary to *the world we live in*. Similarly, the series of articles in the *Journal of Economic Perspectives* discussing observed facts (from tipping in restaurants to interindustry wage differentials) was titled *anomalies*.

price stability and thereby reaping its benefits in terms of economic performance, there is no tradeoff at longer horizons between inflation, on the
one hand, and economic growth or employment, on the other hand, that
can be exploited by monetary policy makers" (Issing 2000: 4). This led to
a consensus that monetary policy's only appropriate objective is to main-
tain price stability, happily appreciated among conservative politicians
and the "fraternity of central bankers" (Tobin 1975). "The main differences among policy-oriented macroeconomists, however, most of whom
seem to accept the concept, is that conservatives tend to put the NAIRU
higher, at say 6.5 or 7 percent, while liberals put it lower, at six or perhaps
5.5 percent" (Eisner 1997: 197). The natural rate of unemployment or
its companion, the Non Accelerating Inflation Rate of Unemployment
(NAIRU),[2] became the yardstick for economic policy.

The simultaneous occurrence of inflation with high and persistent
unemployment (stagflation) in the 1970s was claimed to be evidence
for the failure of Keynesian theory taken as evidence for a vertical
long-run Phillips curve against the "menu of choice" between inflation
and unemployment for governments. "This conclusion is based in part on
the spectacular recent failures of these models and in part on their lack
of a sound theoretical basis" (Lucas & Sargent 1978: 69). For them, it
was a "simple matter of fact, involving no novelties in economic theory"
(Lucas & Sargent 1978: 69). Indeed, the "new" proposals were not new
at all, but the resurrection of the neoclassical model, making unemployment again the result of utility-maximizing choice. Nevertheless, this
resurrection of *homo oeconomicus* was praised as "Theory ahead of the
Facts: Milton Friedman and Edmund Phelps" (Blanchard 1997: 248).
The facts were the "stagflation" in the 1970s cited by Friedman (1976)
in his Nobel Prize Lecture as evidence for his "natural rate theory." This
is a superb example that economists who claim that the only valid test
of a theory is the comparison of its predictions with actual outcomes are
easily satisfied with dubious empirical evidence if their hypotheses seem
to fit the observations. In his Nobel Prize Lecture, Friedman interpreted

---

[2]   Natural rate of unemployment and NAIRU are often used as synonyms, but
as Tobin (1997: 8) explains: "The NAIRU does not assume a Walrasian equilibrium, in which all markets, in particular labor markets, are being cleared by existing prices and wages. [...] The NAIRU is the unemployment rate at which the
inflation increasing effects of the excess-demand markets just balance the inflation decreasing effects of the excess-supply markets. Unlike the natural rate, this
is a balance among disequilibrium markets [...]."

even a short period of stagflation, a vertical Phillips curve, as supporting evidence of his theory. Lucas and Sargent (1978) even claimed that this is proof of the intellectual flaws in Keynes' theory. Stagflation ended in the 1980s, but their theory survived and dominated economic policy among conservatives and infiltrated progressive parties, establishing the widely accepted economic policy conclusion that macroeconomic policy cannot reduce unemployment; the incentive structure must change to favor working over leisure.

Keynesians did not have a ready answer to upward shifts of the Phillips curve (stagflation), although Blinder (1979, 1988) reminded economists that the Phillips tradeoff between unemployment and inflation results from a shift in the labor demand function along with an upward sloping stable supply function. However, a shift of the supply function and a stable demand function results in a positive correlation between unemployment and inflation: stagflation. Thus, supply shocks—like oil-price shocks—can cause a simultaneous rise in inflation and unemployment. Furthermore, rising prices for products with inelastic demand (like oil) may cause inflation and reduce aggregate demand and thus unemployment: stagflation.

Keynesians were not well prepared for the resurrection of the neoclassical labor supply model and its expansion into macroeconomics. Some Keynesians thought microeconomics was not essential for macroeconomic theory and ignored microfoundations or even accepted neoclassical axioms (especially rational choice, maximizing utility and profits) as a good description of economic behavior. To achieve Keynes' underemployment equilibrium, the argument goes, human behavior does not need to diverge from neoclassical assumptions. It is sufficient to recognize some delay in adjustments—some periods of nonoptimal equilibrium—to show the benefits of macroeconomic policy. True, the neoclassical model rests on so many behavioral assumptions, which contrast to *the economy we live in*. However, the success of the neoclassical counterrevolution led to the search for explanations of "imperfect" behavior. In some cases, a more sophisticated utility (profit) maximizing behavior was established, but in others, the impossibility of maximizing and different reasoning was considered. "Why do humans give away money and tip in restaurants?" may illustrate the point: Tipping can be rational and used to "buy" better service for the next visit, but humans tip even if they know that they will never return to the restaurant; it may be simply customary to tip without expecting any returns (Thaler 2015).

Efficiency wage models are a well-known example to recognize "imperfections": Efficiency wages may be paid to reduce turnover costs (Schlicht 1978) or, as in Akerlof and Solow's "sociological models" to positively affect motivation, labor relations etc. Information imperfections lead to signaling (Spence, Stiglitz), Akerlof) and to uncertainty concerning the position and shape of demand and supply functions necessary for optimizing (Stiglitz, Greenwald), habit formation affecting among others labor supply decisions (Clark & Summers) were analyzed by economists as important deviations from the perfect market model. Simultaneously, a group of psychologists (Kahneman, Tversky, Slovic, and others) started experimental research to bridge psychology and economics and investigate the neoclassical model's fundamental assumptions. In cooperation with economists (Frank, Thaler), they established a new branch of economics, Behavioral Economics. Wanner, president of the Russell Sage Foundation, strongly supported this work. Also, in labor economics, several findings questioned the one best recipe, such as Freeman's (2005) "labor market institutions without blinders."

7.2   UNEMPLOYMENT: A UTILITY-MAXIMIZING CHOICE?

How do workers decide whether they participate in the labor market and how many hours they supply? Diverging models of labor supply decisions are the core for classifying unemployment as voluntary—as a utility-maximizing choice—or involuntary due to a limited number of jobs. Keynes' rejected the second postulate of neoclassical economics, namely that workers determine their labor supply in free choice equalizing the marginal disutility of work and the real wage to maximize utility. In other words, he rejected the neoclassical labor supply model, which is a crucial element of Keynes' revolution in economic theory and allowed for involuntary unemployment, for a situation in which workers are constrained through labor demand where the economy is not at its optimal equilibrium. Voluntarily chosen, utility-maximizing unemployment became totally implausible in the 1930s when unemployment rose to 20% and more in a short period. To explain a rise in unemployment by at least 15 percentage points with a sudden shift in preferences—otherwise assumed to be stable in the neoclassical model—in favor of "leisure" was unconvincing. The neoclassical model had and still has no explanation for the level of employment (Keynes 1936, foreword to French edition), which is not determined in the labor market but depends on economic activity in other markets. The economy may fall short of its potential without an automatic mechanism to full employment. Unemployment was no longer simply the result of utility-maximizing choice but was caused by quantity constraints because the economy could balance below the optimum: involuntary unemployment.

Keynes defined full employment from both sides of the labor market, from workers' behavior (labor supply) and the behavior of firms (labor demand). Accepting the first postulate[3] of the neoclassical model, which implies that higher employment requires lower real wages, Keynes had a complicated definition of involuntary unemployment:

> Men are involuntarily unemployed if, in the event of a small rise in the price of wage-goods relatively to the money-wage, both the aggregate supply of labour willing to work for the current money-wage and the aggregate demand for it at that wage would be greater than the existing volume of employment (Keynes 1936: 15).[4]

Therefore, full employment is the absence of involuntary unemployment but allows for frictional and voluntary unemployment. That is some positive unemployment rate in a nonstationary economy where establishments and industries grow and decline, and workers move between establishments (Schettkat 1992).

Keynes also defined full employment in terms of the behavior of labor, "[…] namely a situation in which aggregate employment is inelastic in response to an increase in the effective demand for its output" (Keynes 1936: 26).[5] In other words, full employment is achieved if rising demand does not affect production and employment but only affects prices which is the vertical part of the Phillips curve, the situation in which the rea-

---

[3]   Keynes (1939) seemed to have been less convinced that the first postulate actually holds but by and large he accepted rising marginal costs. Unfortunately, he seemed to have accepted the u-shape marginal cost function common in microeconomics.

[4]   "A small rise in the price of wage goods (consumption goods) relatively to the money wage" indicates that slight inflation at the going money wage leads to an expansion of employment. A decline in the real wage is required because the marginal productivity of labor declines along a neoclassical production at constant capital. In a Phillips curve diagram this translates into a move along the roughly horizontal part of the curve (see below).

[5]   Kahn (1976: 27) reported that in Keynes' view an unemployment rate of 6.5% was "normal" (in September 1930) when the actual unemployment rate was 20%.

soning of the neoclassical model applies. Everybody who wants to work is employed at the going money wage, and production is constrained by capacity, fully used resources, the situation in which the neoclassical conclusions apply. The causation, however, runs from rising product demand to the prices.

The textbook presentation of a labor market shows a downward sloping labor demand function (due to diminishing marginal productivity of labor, first postulate) and an upward sloping labor supply function (straight lines in the left diagram of Figure 7.1). Higher real wages (on the ordinate) lead to lower labor demand but higher labor supply, and vice versa. The labor supply decision can be decomposed into participation and the number of hours supplied. Since time is limited, working competes with leisure. Working provides income, but it reduces the time available for leisure activities. Its opportunity costs—the loss of leisure time—are thought to balance the real wage at the margin.

In the neoclassical labor supply model (see Killingsworth 1983), *homo oeconomicus* maximizes utility and allocates her time to leisure and work so that the marginal utility of leisure equals the real wage. Unemployment results from the individual utility-maximizing choice in the given incentive structures (such as unemployment insurance, taxes, regulations). It is all about choice, commented Eisner (1994), and Rothschild (1993, 1988) asked: "Is there such a thing as unemployment?" At the extremes, all available time is allocated to nonemployment (leisure or unemployment), receiving no earned income (a corner solution), or all time is allocated to work, achieving the maximum income. Well-defined preferences result in convex indifference curves representing all work (income) and leisure combinations where the marginal utility is equal.[6] A preference for income instead of leisure would result in a flat indifference curve, meaning that a small rise in the real wage substantially increases the number of hours worked; the real wage elasticity of labor supply would be high. Steep indifference curves indicate a preference for leisure and to convince workers with steep indifference curves to accept jobs requires paying them higher real wages.

In a neoclassical labor supply model, a higher wage has two consequences: it raises the price of leisure (opportunity costs) and leads to the

---

[6]   Convex indifference curves are identified as rational (because the marginal utility of leisure or income declines with its rise holding the other constant) and guarantee that a linear function is tangential at a unique point, the optimal equilibrium.

substitution of work for leisure (substitution effect). At the same time, the higher income stimulates the desire for more leisure (income effect). Therefore, the net effect of a wage rise on individual labor supply is ambiguous; it depends on the strength of the substitution and the income effect, that is, on the shape of the indifference curve (the preferences). The impact of higher wages on labor supply is not determined in the neoclassical model. However, a rise in unearned income (capital income or transfers) clearly impacts labor supply; it raises the demand for leisure (income effect) and reduces the labor supply.[7] The upward-sloping individual labor supply function in textbook presentations of the labor market results from the assumed dominance of the substitution effect. At the aggregate level, the upward sloping labor supply function displays workers ranked by their reservation wages, the lowest real wage at which nonparticipating workers accept employment. A declining real wage results in some workers leaving their jobs if the real wage falls below their reservation wage; they would prefer unemployment to work because unemployment provides a higher utility.

Keynes observed that workers do not vary their labor supply with the real wage. For this reason, he rejected the second postulate, the neoclassical labor supply model. The labor supply is totally inelastic concerning the real wage. In the real wage labor market diagram, Keynes' labor supply function is vertical (the broken vertical function in the left diagram of Figure 7.1).[8] Accepting real wage reductions but resisting nominal wage reductions is hard for economists adhering to the principles of logic to swallow. A money wage reduction of 10% but constant prices is similar to a constant nominal wage at 10% inflation; anything else is illogical, simply "money illusion." However, in a decentralized economy, wages are not determined at the macro level and any change in money wages may affect the relative wage probably most relevant in decentralized wage bargaining (see Trevithick 1976). But as Keynes explained and Behavioral Economics confirms, it is not as illogical as one might think because humans are socially embedded and care about relative wages, and nominal values serve as a reference. Nominal wage

---

[7]   The corner solution would hit the indifference curve at a steeper part and thus requires a higher real wage to decide for working.

[8]   This characterization, however, will apply to a certain range of real wages, since most workers rely on their earned income and a sharp decline in the real wage may cause an inverse reaction leading to higher rather than lower labor supply.

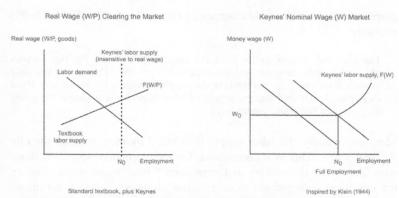

Standard textbook, plus Keynes

Inspired by Klein (1944)

Note: The upward sloping labor supply function displayed in textbooks depends on real wages (W/P). It can be derived from individual labor supply, assuming that the substitution effect dominates the income effect or that workers are sorted according to their real reservation wage. Keynes argued that labor supply is inelastic to variation in the real wage resulting in a vertical labor supply function in real wage-employment space. This is undoubtedly an exaggeration because he made his argument of insensitivity, not for the whole range of wages. However, most likely, the supply decision will be inverse at some point when workers need to extend their supply to achieve a minimum income.

Figure 7.1   Neoclassical and Keynes' labor market

reduction in a decentralized economy cannot secure the relative position, but inflation affects everybody. Furthermore, money wages serve as reference points affecting workers' motivation but some commentators argue that Keynes introduced nominal wage rigidity not to describe behavior but as a policy suggestion because falling nominal wages may not reduce but rather increase unemployment because labor demand is derived from product demand which may decline with nominal wages (as brilliantly explained in Chapter 19 of the *General Theory*).

In his dissertation, supervised by Samuelson at MIT, Klein (1944)[9] developed from workers' resistance to money wage reduction and Keynes' definition of involuntary unemployment (that workers are prepared to accept jobs for the going money wage (W_0)) the labor market

---

[9]   Klein was awarded the Nobel Prize in 1980 "for the creation of econometric models and the application to the analysis of economic fluctuations and economic policies" (Nobel Prize Committee).

graph presented in the right diagram of Figure 7.1. Klein (1944: 88–89) explains:

> The classical system would have the equation $N = f(W/P)$; But Keynes objected to this equation and substituted $N = F(W)$. This is not the only modification which he has made in the supply schedule, for he has also fixed its shape. He has said that the supply of labor is perfectly elastic at the going wage up to a full employment level.

Most importantly, the labor supply is affected by money rather than by the real wage. This is a conundrum for many economists, even those who like to see themselves as Keynesians.[10] Real wage orientation, on the one hand, is ingrained in economists' thinking, but in a decentralized bargaining system, employment contracts are defined in money terms and provide a basis for ranking. Workers cannot bargain over real wages (Hahn & Solow 1986). Money wage cuts, on the other hand, would leave open whether reference groups experienced similar cuts. Rising consumer prices would not change relative wages and negotiating real wages[11] would be difficult since changes in consumer prices affect workers who may face inflation different from their employer's product prices. Klein explained that "The shape of the functions of the Keynesian system is not, by any means, solely determined by a few partial derivatives. It is necessary to inquire further into what lies behind some of these schedules" (Klein 1944: 86). Entrepreneurial spirit, the joy of doing something, is excluded from the neoclassical model in which utility is related only to the outcome of work—income—but work itself is regarded as a burden. In Klein's graph, full employment is achieved at N_0 when the labor supply response to nominal wage rises becomes elastic.

---

[10]   Some argue that Keynes needed a rigidity to achieve non-clearing markets but nominal wage rigidity was not meant as a description of behavior but rather for conclusion for economic policy. Flexible nominal wages would not result in proportionally declining real wages because with wage costs also prices will fall but demand may suffer, resulting in an overall negative demand and employment effect.

[11]   Carlin and Soskice (1990) and Layard, Nickell and Jackman (1991) developed models in which unions and employer's associations negotiate expected real wages.

However, the male labor supply is inelastic in the industrialized world, but substantial changes occurred among women.[12] Interpreting the totally elastic horizontal part of the labor supply function in Klein's graph means that a slight decline in the money wage leads to a complete withdrawal of the labor supply. Do workers quit their jobs if their money wages decline? Do they have that choice? Most workers rely on their earned income, and quitting into unemployment is no option, even if unemployment benefits are available. Quitting is procyclical: high in tight labor markets and low in recessions. A person does not need to be unemployed to be looking for a new job. Once a better job is found, workers quit. Searching while unemployed may send negative signals in a market with imperfect and asymmetric information (Spence 1973), setting a strong incentive to search while still employed. There are "good jobs" and "bad jobs,"[13] and quitting is significantly higher at the latter when tight labor markets create a mobility chain (Schettkat 1996a). In addition, it is easier for workers to correct their decisions and leave an unsatisfactory job in a tight labor market because they can find a better one. Furthermore, in tight labor markets, quits initiate hiring efforts because firms will likely replace the departed worker. Depending on the tightness of the labor market, a whole hiring chain is formed, allowing for minor skill adjustments (Schettkat 1994, 1996a, 1996b).

Although workers' resistance to money wage cuts is plausible, it was perplexing why employers do not pay less in recessions on their workforce or simply replace their employees with unemployed workers. Employment contracts usually define inputs (hours), but effort and engagement are relevant for employers, which was investigated under the labeling efficiency wage theory. Motivation and fairness are especially relevant in the social efficiency wage models of Akerlof and Solow (Akerlof 1982; Akerlof & Yellen 1986; Solow 1979). Bewley (1995, 1999) showed that workers' productivity would be negatively affected by cuts in money wages. In contrast, a fair money wage improves motivation and reduces quits (Schettkat 1993). Krueger and Mas (2003) found that defective tires increase if labor disputes in tire manufacturing facilities are left unresolved.

---

[12] Labor supply of women is elastic but men show inelastic supply (Killingsworth 1983: 104).

[13] "Bad jobs" are jobs in low paying industries (as in Krueger & Summers 1987, 1988).

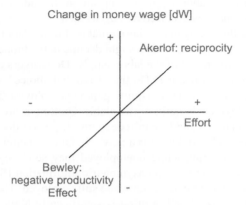

Figure 7.2   *Effort function of money wage changes*

What determines the full employment position (N_0 in Figure 7.1, right diagram)? "At the going wage" clearly refers to the short-run when habits, traditions, and educational levels are presumably fixed. Empirical studies have suggested that history (reference points) is essential. Education substantially affects female participation in the labor force, most likely driven by the desire to use their skills and earn an income (Freeman & Schettkat 2005, Schettkat & Yocarini 2001). It is probably impossible to disentangle the effects of income potential and the desire to use skills, and the two variables are best regarded as a process.

The "new microeconomics," where the "new" stands for relaxing the perfect information assumption, gave the proponents a revolutionary feeling (Phelps 1970). Job mobility and searching became fashionable to explain unemployment, searching for new jobs while unemployed. The assumption was that job searching takes time and is best done from unemployment. In Phelps' island parable, the unemployed are rowing from one information island to another to collect wage information. How long do they row? They row until the gains in wages equal the costs of searching. One may know the costs, but how does one know the potential wage gains of continued searching? This requires knowing the wage distribution. However, how does one evaluate whether one found the best alternative jobs? Even if one assumes that wages are known, jobs have more than one relevant characteristic, and many are unobservable externally. For sure, unemployed workers search, but most job searches for new jobs are done while employed, preventing the stigma of unemployment. Potential employers have little information on the applicant's productivity, and therefore unemployment—especially long-term unemployment—may signal lower productivity (Spence 1973) in normal times when unemployment is more likely related to personal characteristics compared to recessions when the risk of becoming unemployed is less selective but general. Actually, hiring from among the unemployed rises in recessions (Schettkat 1994).

Unemployment benefits allow for longer searches, but most workers search while employed and quit once they find a more suitable job without any unemployment spells. Does the job search crowd out unemployed job seekers (Burgess 1993)? Employed and unemployed job seekers compete for specific jobs, but in the aggregate, only the ratio of vacant positions to unemployed workers is relevant (Gorter & Schettkat 2009). If employed workers quit their job, they most likely leave a vacancy behind. Therefore they do not crowd out unemployed job seekers; instead, they may initiate a hiring and mobility chain in tight labor markets, opening opportunities for minor skill adjustments. Comparing the unemployed workers' skills with those required at the vacant positions may show a skill discrepancy. This skill mismatch is often interpreted as structural unemployment that cannot be tackled by stimulating macroeconomic policy. Still, in upswings, even the "unemployable" find jobs (Rothschild 1993, Diamond, 2010), not least because lower unemployment in the upswing initiates job-to-job mobility, a hiring chain also facilitating skill adjustments (Russo, Gorter & Schettkat 2001, Schettkat 1994).

7.3   THEORY CONFIRMED BY VAGUE EVIDENCE? NOBEL CONFUSION

Friedman famously argued that theories could not be judged by the validity of their axioms but only by comparing predictions with outcomes (positive economics). However, the emphasis on strong internal consistency may lead researchers to interpret empirical results too quickly and probably wrongly to support their theory; theory may work as blinders. It seems that Friedman became a victim of this fallacy. In his Nobel Prize Lecture, Friedman (1976) celebrated his natural rate theory and argued that the downward-sloping Phillips curve was a transitory phenomenon because the economy returns to the optimal equilibrium, the natural rate. Expansionary macroeconomic policy pushes the labor market (the economy) away from its optimal equilibrium and initiates inflation; unemployed workers will leave their maximal utility position only for higher real wages, but at the same time, the marginal productivity of the additional workers will be lower this way creating price pressure.

Friedman claimed that workers' short-term labor supply reactions to expansionary macroeconomic policy produce the downward-sloping Phillips curve. But these reactions are simply mistakes, a confusion of money wage increases with real wage increases. Once workers discover their error, they return to their initial position, the utility optimum. In the long run, the Phillips curve will be vertical at the "natural rate of unemployment." What looks like a Phillips curve in high-frequency data (say annual data) will disappear in low-frequency data (say five-year periods) when short-run deviations cancel. The corrective mechanism to the "natural rate of unemployment," Friedman argued, did not spring into the economists' minds earlier because Phillips' original data covered a period with "[...] a relatively stable long-run price level and when the expectations of continued stability were widely shared" (Friedman 1976: 282). Phillips' analysis, however, was based on British data for a substantial period from 1861 to 1957 with the unemployment rate (from 1% to 11%) and changes in money wages from -3% to +9%; usually not regarded as a time of exceptional stability.[14]

For presentation in his Nobel Prize Lecture, Friedman averaged inflation and unemployment rates for five-year periods[15] of seven countries (Italy, France, Japan, Sweden, UK, USA, and Germany) from the mid-1950s to the early 1970s (as displayed in the upper graph of Figure 7.3, which is the original Figure 3 of Friedman's published lecture; reprinted with the kind permission of the Nobel Prize Committee). Indeed, since the early 1960s, both the unemployment and inflation rates rose together, with a steep rise from 1966–1970 to 1971–1975 and interpreted as confirmation of the theoretically deduced vertical Phillips curve and taken as evidence that expansionary macroeconomic policy can create inflation but not employment.

The neoclassical model assumes an unbiased perception of the world, and therefore the presentation of data should be irrelevant, but a careful look at the Friedman graph may create some irritations. The impression

---

[14]   Phillips estimated a function with data from 1861 to 1913 and used the second part of his sample to analyze the fit.

[15]   It appears that the averaging over five-year periods is not very important. In the extended period the coefficient of correlation between inflation and unemployment is -0.51 for the five-year averages even slightly higher than in the annual data (-0.48).

of a close simultaneous rise of inflation and unemployment since the end 1960s is exaggerated in Friedman's presentation because he used an expanded scale for the unemployment rates and shifted the scale up. The lower chart in Figure 7.3 reproduces the Friedman graph with his data until 1971–1975 (grey-shaded area) but put inflation and unemployment on the same scale and position. The positive correlation between the inflation and unemployment series is still visible, but it no longer gives the impression of a very close co-variation of inflation and unemployment as the original graph. Instead, it seems that inflation runs away from unemployment in the late 1960s to early 1970s, which causes questions about the reasons for inflation in that period (see below). These and other problems with the composition and averaging across a group of countries aside, Friedman based the proof of the neoclassical unique equilibrium theory on three data points. A fabulous illustration that emphasizes the internal consistency of a theory may work as blinders and that framing influences conclusions. A few data points fitting the theory's prediction are sufficient evidence for the unique equilibrium "natural rate theory?"[16] Lucas and Sargent (1978) went even further and took stagflation in the 1970s as evidence that stagflation disproved the Keynesian model.

They claimed that workers are "fooled into employment" if confronted with the macroeconomic policy the first time, but that they will learn that it results in inflation and will not repeat the mistakes; they will form rational expectations. Lucas and Sargent (1978: 65) state: "Employers and workers are fooled into too many jobs by unexpected inflation, but only until they learn it affects other prices, not just the prices of what they sell. The reverse happens temporarily when inflation falls short of expectation." Learning was already in Phelps' (1967) reasoning on the upward shifting Phillips curve, but learning is used as a substitute for discovering the static neoclassical model Lucas and others had in mind.[17] If economic agents only had all the necessary information, they would perfectly estimate the pertinent relative prices (ratios of real values).

---

[16]   The theoretically deduced vertical Phillips curve should be even more visible in 10 years averages of inflation and unemployment rates but it does not show up. Theoretical and empirical research in economics is strongly influenced by analysis on the US which comes closest to a vertical Phillips curve, but averaged over decades the US unemployment rates range from 5% (1960s) to around 7% (1980s). Although a 2 percentage points difference in average unemployment rates is not negligible, Taylor (2000) argued that it roughly fits natural rate theory.

[17]   For summaries of "learning": Lam (2016), Zhen (2015).

Interaction among agents is simply reduced to symmetric deviations from the average (the representative agent).

> In particular, under certain conditions, agents will tend temporarily to mistake a general increase in all absolute prices as an increase in the relative price of the good that they are selling, leading them to increase their supply of that good over what they had previously planned. Since everyone is, on average, making the same mistake, aggregate output will rise above what it would have been. (Lucas & Sargent 1978: 60)

This is a remarkable statement: General prices rise, but agents perceive higher prices as higher real demand for their specific good? Indeed, an astonishingly passive view on management, prices rise first, and agents react; but who raises prices? Price signals are essential but not the only signals; management surely will monitor orders which actually may be the first signal received.

Since there are short-term effects on production and employment when macroeconomic stimulation is applied initially, what do economic agents learn when they react to expansionary macroeconomic policy for the first time? Economic agents will not respond to expansionary macroeconomic policy after learning that there is no tradeoff between unemployment and inflation. The Phillips curve will be vertical even in the short run. Learning in Lucas (1986), however, is simply a metaphor for discovering his static equilibrium model, which he assumes is the true model. Abstracting from time and the sequential events, the "true" relations will be found, but if in historical time agents may instead learn that macroeconomic impulses led to an expansion of production, that the economy changed its path, achieving a higher equilibrium and probably full employment.

Extending the Friedman chart to the recent years for the same set of countries and five-year averages with the data from the Ameco database[18] shows no support for the "natural rate theory" anymore. On the contrary, from the 1980s on, a decline in inflation from about 9.5% to less than 2% occurred but was accompanied by a sharp rise in unemployment following the Phillips curve pattern. Most important, unemployment remained at a high level in the average of the seven countries. Especially France and Germany experienced very low unemployment of around 1% and an inflation rate of just over 2% in the 1960s. At this time, the

---

[18]   Germany is up to 1990 West Germany, thereafter united Germany.

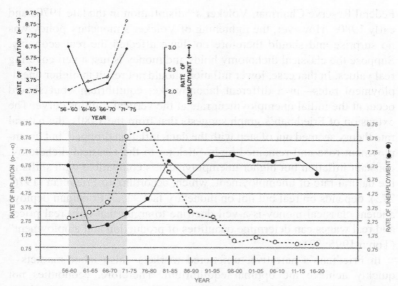

Note: Lower Graph: data points 1956–1975 (grey shaded area in the lower graph) from Friedman, after that year calculations are based on the Ameco Database, unweighted five-year averages of unemployment rates and Consumer Price Index (CPI) of the same seven countries as in Friedman's original graph. Note that unemployment is scaled and positioned similar to inflation in the lower chart. Countries: Italy, France, Japan, Sweden, UK, USA, Germany (until 1990 West Germany, after that united Germany).
Source: Upper graph from Friedman (1976), Figure 3, reprinted with permission of the Nobel Prize Committee.

Figure 7.3   *Unemployment and inflation, Friedman's Nobel lecture and extension*

Council of Economic Advisors (1962) wondered why European unemployment was so much lower than in the US, but in the 1980s and 1990s, unemployment in France and Germany exceeded the US unemployment rate.[19] The changing trends after 1980 can be a policy response, in the sense that governments and/or central banks put greater weight on low inflation and anchoring expectations of inflation as often associated with

---

[19]   Remarkably the decade average of the inflation rates in the 1970s in Germany was only about 5% and was in the 1980s down to the level of the 1960s but with sharply higher unemployment rates (around 6% instead of less than 1% in the 1960s).

Federal Reserve Chairman Volcker's[20] disinflation in the late 1970s and early 1980s. However, the tightening of Volcker's monetary policy was no surprise and should therefore not have affected the real economy. Suppose the classical dichotomy holds and money is just a veil covering real values. In that case, lower inflation should not result in higher unemployment rates—in a different labor market equilibrium—but should occur at the initial unemployment rate at the vertical Phillips curve. The extension of Friedman's graph suggests that from the 1980s, the natural rate theory seemed out of step with the data, inflation dropped, but unemployment rose and remained high. Sticking to the classical dichotomy, constant inflation but higher unemployment is compatible with shifts in the natural rate of unemployment, which, according to Friedman (1976: 273), depends on real but not on monetary fact. "[…] Friedman deploys ancient classical money-is-a-veil doctrine to argue that only real prices and real wages can determine quantities of production and employment" (Tobin 1995: 32).

In Friedman's narrative, unfettered markets—also labor markets—quickly achieve the optimal equilibrium. Therefore, economies not returning to the initial equilibrium—to their natural rate—must have experienced a change in real factors affecting the natural unemployment rate. Such real factors could have been labor market regulations (e.g., employment protection), labor market dynamics, structural change (mismatch), insider-outsider wage setting, and, of course, the incentive structure to work. Higher European unemployment, so the conclusion according to this narrative, needed to be sought in institutional factors. For example, more generous unemployment benefits (easier access, longer benefit durations) may lead to longer job searches.[21] But to explain rising European unemployment as "natural" with more generous labor market measures does not fit the time scheme; "timing is wrong" (Solow 2000). Actually, institutional reforms should have lowered the natural rate in Germany (Carlin & Soskice 2008). Nevertheless, the astonishing conclusion was that the theory holds but that the natural rates shifted upwards. Therefore, Europe needed to deregulate—especially the labor

---

[20]   Volcker (Volcker & Harper 2018) was chairman of the Fed from 1979 to 1987 and committed to a tight monetary policy.
[21]   Demographics may also shift natural rates of employment (see Katz & Krueger 1999).

markets—and reform its welfare state institutions, which were most influential in the OECD's Jobs Study (1994).

Although Friedman's natural rate relation was short-lived in the data, it survived in economics and became the anchor for numerous econometric exercises and policy recommendations. After the 1980s, the relationship between inflation and unemployment rates—the Phillips curve—became roughly horizontal; various unemployment rates occurred at approximately constant inflation rates (Brainard & Perry 2001, Kromphardt & Logeay 2011, Stock & Watson 2019).[22] A vertical Phillips curve should appear in data covering more extended periods, such as Friedman's five-year average or even better ten-year average.[23] But where is the natural rate if the Phillips curve flattens, implying that very different unemployment rates occur at stable inflation rates?[24] One interpretation for a flat Phillips curve is that the economy is simply at the flat part of the Phillips curve and that inflation is caused by a mechanism other than the overuse of resources. In other words, the natural rate estimates may have misguided economic policy.

It was largely ignored in the economic debate that welfare state arrangements and regulations are not the only institutional differences between Europe and the US. Monetary policy and fiscal policy differed substantially and allowed the US to return to former unemployment rates after recessions. In contrast, Europe had balanced budget rules and a restrictive asymmetric monetary policy, first by the Bundesbank and then by the European Central Bank, which slowed unemployment to return to prerecession levels (Schettkat & Sun 2009). Germany and, with it, Europe suffered from overly tight asymmetric monetary policy and balanced budget programs. The economic policy debate became unnecessarily narrow and one-sided and should be broadened (Solow 2008).

---

[22] Gordon (2013) argues that his triangle model still allows to identify a Phillips Curve and compute a NAIRU, which is needed as a reference for economic policy. It is one of the three stars.

[23] Other forms of averaging such as moving averages or filtering may also be used.

[24] Gagnon (2017) from the Peterson Institute argues in line with Phillips (1958) that the slope of the Phillips curve disappears at very low rates of inflation (below 3%) because of downward price rigidity which eliminates the negative price changes at low inflation rates.

7.4   CAUSES FOR INFLATION AND STAGFLATION

Stimulating the economy beyond full employment will cause rising prices, but the reverse conclusion that inflation (rising inflation) indicates the full or over use of resources is misleading. What causes inflation? In the natural rate narrative, the economy is assumed to be at full employment; real wages are consistent with individual utility maximization of workers; those who do not work are voluntarily unemployed; to attract them into jobs requires higher real wages, but at the same time, the real wage is assumed to equal the marginal productivity of labor which diminishes with rising employment. Consequently, the neoclassical model predicts that higher nominal wage offers cannot turn into real wages. Inflation will reduce the real value of nominal wage rises. Therefore, assuming the economy and unemployment as well as employed workers in their optimal equilibrium together with the neoclassical production function must result in inflation. At full employment, a macroeconomic stimulus destroys the equilibrium everybody regarded as optimal and pushes the economy beyond its capacity beyond full employment. Workers were fooled into employment by the illusion that higher money wages are higher real wages.

For Friedman (1956: 4) "inflation is always and everywhere a monetary phenomenon"; the economy is pushed out of equilibrium into an unsustainable situation unless another dose of expansionary policy pushes it to even higher inflation rates. Keynes (1936: 5) accepted the marginal productivity theory of wages (the second neoclassical postulate); unfortunately, as Tobin remarks because it requires declining real wages to increase employment which is achieved through a slight rise in the price of consumption goods. "For a given money stock, adjustments in relative prices are accomplished through increases in some nominal prices and decreases of others" Friedman 1975: 73). Although capital may be optimally used in the long run, this is hardly the case in a recession if the economy is at a suboptimal equilibrium, if the economy is below the full use of its capacity and most likely below full use of capital. If the economy falls into recession, capital will be idle, and the marginal productivity of labor is unlikely to decline in the expansion.[25] Keynes

---

[25]   Schumpeter (1939) argued that the business cycle is caused by structural changes from old to innovative industries. Preventing this change will slow inno-

was confronted with the empirical work of two economists—Dunlop (1938) and Tarshis (1939)—who found that real wages move in conjunction with output, contradicting the need for lower real wages to expand employment. Keynes (1939) seems to have accepted the Dunlop and Tarshis intervention for the short term with some skepticism. "When the facts change, I change my mind. What do you do, Sir?" is apocryphally ascribed to Keynes because it reflects Keynes' undoctrinaire attitude. At least in a recession, when capital is idle, the marginal labor productivity may not fall but rise with expanding production and employment.

Is the economy fully using its potential? What is the production potential of an economy? One way to estimate potential production is to use a structural model, but another more common method is to use trends for the estimates. If the economy is assumed to use resources optimally, the average over some period or the trend would be a reasonable estimate for the potential. However, if one allows for underemployment equilibria, these averages are biased, and trends may be wrong. Okun (1981) argued that the potential needs to be estimated using only the years when the economy is at full employment; otherwise, the estimated capacity will be underestimated.[26] Natural rate theory uses unemployment to determine the potential, assuming that inflation should be stable in equilibrium. If inflation occurs, the economy is classified as above full employment. Although price pressure arises when resources are overused, the reverse conclusion that inflation indicates that the economy is beyond its potential is invalid. There are other sources of inflation, especially in the 1970s when prices of natural resources—the oil price shocks—spiked.[27]

Hamilton's data (2011, Table 1) shows that the 1973–1974 oil price hikes were similar to the price increases in 2007–2008 but without the severe effects on inflation and unemployment.

This seems to support Friedman's assertion that only relative prices matter and that therefore inflation is always and everywhere a monetary

---

vation and therefore one should let recessions do their job (for critical comment: Krugman 2021).

[26] See Horn, Logeay and Tober (2007) for an overview of estimation methods.

[27] Many more things happened in the early 1970s: food shortages occurred, Nixon first initiated and then gradually relaxed wage and price controls, the Bretton Woods system of fixed exchange rates broke down after the official withdrawal of the convertibility of the US dollar into gold followed by a devaluation of the US dollar.

phenomenon[28]. If the monetary price of one product rises, other products' prices will decline given that that the stock of money is held constant. Furthermore, the price of oil rose already in the 1960s, well before the oil price shocks (along similar lines: Kilian 2008). Arguments in line with Friedman's assertion that only relative prices are relevant. If the monetary price of one product rises, other products' prices will decline given that that the stock of money is held constant. Obviously, Friedman's assertion relies on a high elasticity of substitution among various products, shifting demand to substitutes with declining relative prices. In the neoclassical model, real factors determine relative prices, which steer markets to equilibrium; the price level depends on money supply; the classical dichotomy (see, e.g., Ball & Mankiw 1992). In other words, money is a veil for relative prices which steer the economy to equilibrium. The money veil may cause confusion in the short run but not in the long run; monetary policy cannot affect production and employment; it is neutral to output and employment.

However, the Fed's response to the oil price hikes in the early 1970s was a restrictive monetary policy to face inflationary pressure, accounting for two-thirds to three-fourths of the total effect of the oil price shock on output (Bernanke, Gertler & Watson 1997). They conclude that "an important part of the effect of oil price shocks on the economy results not from the change in oil prices, per se, but from the resulting tightening of monetary policy" (136). At least in the short run, the price elasticity of demand for oil is inelastic because no substitutes were available. In addition, OPEC raised the price of oil and restricted quantities supplied, causing an inward shift of the oil-supply function, which is the essential difference between the two periods of rising oil prices in the 1970s and 2000s (see Hamilton 2011). Restrictive monetary and fiscal policies reined in inflation (Blinder 1979) and the effect of the oil-price hike of the 1970s on overall demand in the US economy and other industrialized countries, given inelastic demand for oil, is like an excise tax where the revenue went to OPEC or other oil producers. In both cases, it results in redistribution "[...] expected to reduce aggregate demand because the

---

[28]   De Grauwe and Polan (2005) found with a large dataset (160 countries over 30 years) that Friedman's relationship between money supply and inflation cannot be confirmed if the data is restricted to countries with "normal" inflation—less than 10% per year. It also seems that price dispersion—the alleged economic costs of inflation—are not varying with inflation (Nakamura et al. 2018).

groups 'collecting' the 'excise taxes' have lower propensities to spend than the groups paying the 'taxes'" (Blinder 1979: 39). Thus, rising oil prices but inelastic demand for oil created both inflation and a decline in aggregate demand, leaving economic policy between two bad choices, either to stimulate the economy and accept inflation or accept a recession and rising unemployment.

Studies on the impact of monetary policy on output often have a built-in tendency to equilibrium imposing long-run neutrality of monetary impulses but find "short-run" effects between four (Bernanke & Gertler 1995) and ten years (Bernanke & Mihov 1998). Mankiw (2000), commenting on Bernanke and Mihov, argued that without a prior, "The data's best guess is that monetary shocks leave permanent scars on the economy" (6). In a meta-analysis of 86 studies, de Grauwe and Costa Storti (2008: 48) find that "[...] in those econometric studies that do not impose long-run neutrality, the long-run neutrality of money is rejected." In general, statistical tests reject the null hypothesis (the theory's predictions) only if the probability for observed parameters under the Null (H0) is very low; to keep the theory unless the evidence for the counter hypothesis (H1) is very strong. This approach is viable if the evidence for the theory is very strong, but the hypothesis of neutrality of monetary policy rests on assumptions contradicted by Behavioral Economics experiments. Hysteresis theories of unemployment, of course, predict long-lasting effects even of otherwise short-run impacts of monetary policy (see Ball 2009). In their empirical analysis of every US business cycle since 1950, Romer and Romer (1994) conclude that monetary policies, when enacted early, can counter recessions. Blinder and Reis (2005) give monetary policy credit for the extended US growth period in the 1990s. Theoretically, owing to short-run wage or price rigidities, changes in the money supply might induce a short-run tradeoff between inflation and unemployment. Alternatively, some economists explore real rigidities to explain the non-neutralities of money (see Ball & Romer 1990; Solow 1985). The public was apprised of the disinflation Volcker initiated in the late 1970s and early 1980s; it was by no means a surprise. Therefore, under the neutrality hypothesis of monetary policy, it should not have affected the real economy, but it caused a severe rise in unemployment (B. Friedman 1984).

Reflecting on his experiences as Fed chairman during the Great Recession (2008–2009), Bernanke (2015) seems to have changed his view on the long-run neutrality of monetary policy when he argues that the more active response of the Fed in comparison to the European

Central Bank (ECB) led to substantially different growth rates and diverging unemployment. He argues that the very long-run consequences of the ECB's reluctant monetary policy are most severe for unemployed young people who are hoping to begin their careers but who are cut off from developing their potential, which has long-term adverse effects on economic growth.

8. Conclusion: the economy we live in

Keynes' *General Theory* is regarded as the birth of macroeconomics. Still, its microfoundations were (are) neglected mainly, although these are the basis for his fundamental conclusion that economies may balance at suboptimal equilibria without any endogenous mechanism to full employment, the optimum; the economy may get stuck in a suboptimal equilibrium—underemployment. Therefore, macroeconomic policies can improve the economy's welfare; a sharp distinction between Keynes' theory and the neoclassical model in which maximizing individuals exploit all opportunities until the welfare optimum (full employment) is achieved. Maximization and equilibrium are the essential neoclassical microfoundations declared to be the only basis for good economic theory from which everything else can be logically deduced. Not accepting neoclassical microfoundations led to the accusation that Keynes' theory is intellectually flawed. Still, his revolution shifted the criterium of good economic theory from the consistency with axioms (maximization, optimal equilibrium) to the consistency with *the economy we live in* at the micro and macro level. The accusation that Keynes' theory misses microfoundations altogether or that it is laypeople economics is itself flawed. Keynes' macroeconomic conclusions are based on observed microeconomic actions of humans as entrepreneurs, workers, consumers, and investors in a monetary economy, impressively confirmed by the rigorous research in Behavioral Economics applying several methods (observations, interviews, experiments, neurological analysis). Both Keynes and Behavioral Economics require "good economic theory" to be externally consistent—descriptive—with the abilities and actions of humans in *the economic environment we live in*. The methodological orientation of Behavioral Economics and Keynes is that of real science, which requires an empirical content of the behavioral assertions. This is no less than a fundamental shift in the requirement of good economic theory, a methodological revolution.

The different methodological approaches of Keynes and Behavioral Economics on the one side and the neoclassical model on the other have severe consequences for the research programs and methods. Keynes' theory and Behavioral Economics contrast the axiomatic approach of neoclassical economics, which claims that assumptions are axioms, instrumental, obvious, and "true" without proof. For neoclassical economists science begins with logical deductions from the premises (internal consistency). Rational choice, picking the utility-maximizing among the myriad of options, is obvious? Actually, it hinges on so many assumptions of motivation, perception, the economic environment, and others that it surely needs justification. Behavioral Economics produced a stunning amount of studies over the last decades showing that economic agents are humans who change preferences, develop habits, are socially embedded, make mistakes, and others more.

Hahn and Solow (1986)—as Keynes before—asked the "blasphemous" question, "Is wage flexibility a good thing?" challenging the assertion that price variations clear (labor) markets. Keynes even challenged the sine qua non of good economic theory (Akerlof & Yellen 1987), namely that individuals decide rationally. Rational economic agents are supposed to maximize their own utility along with their preferences subject to a budget constraint, optimization. Individuals calculate the expected values of the various combinations of expected utilities (profits, respectively) and probabilities, rank them and pick the top-ranked, the maximum. Keynes accused the "orthodox theory" that "The hypothesis of a calculable future leads to a wrong interpretation of the principles of behavior which the need for action compels us to adopt, and to an underestimation of the concealed factors of utter doubt, precariousness, hope and fear" (Keynes 1937: 222). The entrepreneur's production and investment decisions today depend on expected future demand and profits, which, in turn, affects today's employment, labor income, and aggregate demand (effective demand). Under uncertainty, expectations cannot be rational, because expected values cannot be computed as under risk. Instability may occur because all decisions are future-oriented and depend on expectations.

How do entrepreneurs, investors, workers, and consumers decide under uncertainty? They collect information on the pros and cons of (some) options, which improves their confidence, but uncertainty remains. The final decision cannot be based on calculations but depends on emotions and animal spirits, arguably next to nominal wage orientation in labor supply, one of the most disputed elements of Keynes' theory. However,

Schumpeter's celebrated hero, the innovative entrepreneur, cannot possibly be rational because they pioneer unknown, uncertain territory for which no probability distributions exist. The entrepreneurial spirit in Schumpeter's narrative is based on hope, sentiment, and the urge and desire to do but not on cold calculations of rational choice. Emotions affecting decisions are impossible to accept for neoclassical economists and even for many Keynesians. But recent progress in neurological research applying so-called functional magnetic resonance imaging (fMRI) identified different brain regions active in decision processes and found that emotions are involved in every decision, sometimes in competition with the cognitive system, which seems unable to decide in isolation.

However, the feeling remained that somehow future-oriented decisions can be calculated. Although the knowledge of probabilities required for rational choice is lagging, decisions are made; subjective probability—the individual's guess—was invented to formally fit the theory. Subjective probability substituted true probabilities in the maximization equation in an effort to rescue the rationality axiom. Subjective probability keeps the algebra formally intact, but a guessed subjective probability seems just to be another word for emotions and animal spirits. The roulette gambler who puts all his money on red because it did not pop up for so long obviously calculates the expected value based on a very high subjective probability for red; nevertheless, he may be frustrated or even ruined after the next draw. Ellsberg's experiments showed that humans lag the required consistent behavior necessary for rational choice; they switch preferences under uncertainty. Managers confronted with experiments of the Ellsberg type also changed preferences and violated rational choice. However, after explanations that they violated the rationality axiom, they did not correct their choices which were no mistakes but expressing genuine preferences.

The rigorous research of Behavioral Economics produced innumerous findings showing that moods and circumstances affect decisions, the framing of options influences decisions, losses are valued different from gains (prospect theory), evaluation depends on reference points, social norms, relative positions, heuristics—rules of thumb—rather than cold calculations. Preferences are far from stable: the possession of a product changes its valuation (endowment effect), buying and asking prices deviate, expected utility often differs from experienced utility, habits develop. Axioms are powerful in structuring our thinking, but many paradoxes are only paradoxes if the rationality axiom holds. Nevertheless, some Behavioral Economists claim that their findings extend the neoclassical model, making it more realistic, although most results show that human decisions violate the neoclassical axioms.

Unfettered markets are claimed to coordinate decentralized individual decisions to the welfare maximum (optimum), but where is the optimum? When do individuals reach their utility optimum? Rational choice does not determine what to choose; it is a method, Becker explained. But what actually is the method? The method is the axiomatic approach which assumes consistent, maximizing decisions, and therefore observed choices are declared as maxima. As long as utility remains unmeasured, the claim is impossible to prove. However, a theory that predicts the economy to use its resources fully and achieve full employment does not need macroeconomic stimulation; it even pushes the economy away from the equilibrium. Nobody has ever shown that actual outcomes are optimal (Simon); declaring realized situations as optima because that is what the theory predicts can hardly convince the skeptic.

Many Keynesian economists shied away from microeconomic analysis allowing neoclassical axioms to dominate microeconomic thinking; microfoundations even became synonymous for neoclassical axioms. However, the perfect market model is too extreme. A new consensus developed where some economists accept that adjustments need time (short-run deviations from the optimum), and others take rational expectation (Wren-Lewis 2007). Some obvious rigidities such as staggered contracts or menu costs were made compatible with rational behavior. Prices do not react instantaneously, and the market may therefore not clear immediately and therefore maximization requires taking the cost of price changes into account. This way, the congruence with rationality may be saved, but it cannot counter the argument that uncertainty about demand reactions (Stiglitz) makes entrepreneurs reluctant to change prices.

Following the logic of the axiomatic approach seems to result in asymmetric skepticism: Empirical results compatible with outcomes deduced from the axioms are quickly interpreted as "strong" evidence in favor of the theory. Friedman's Nobel Lecture is a prime example; some data points convinced him that his natural rate hypothesis was valid, and the natural rate of unemployment became the new full employment. Although celebrated as "theory ahead of the facts," it was "old wine in new bottles," and the facts (stagflation) supporting the hypothesis were short-lived. The theory—a revival of unemployment as a voluntary utility-maximizing choice—shifted economic policy away from

Keynesian macroeconomics to neoclassical (supply-side) microeconomics, the incentive structure, and consequently, the reform of institutional arrangements (welfare state institutions, regulations).

On the other hand, Card and Krueger's (1995) finding based on a natural experiment that minimum wage legislation does not necessarily result in massive job losses was criticized because empirical work cannot identify the causal effects of specific policy interventions. The interactions in the economy are too complex; causal effects can only be identified in formal models (Flinn 2010). Demanding caution when interpreting empirical studies seems relevant, but economic complexity is the reason for doubts that humans can choose rationally (to maximize) in complex situations (Simon). However, the important methodological contribution of Behavioral Economics (psychology, actually) is carefully designed controlled experiments. One may argue that people behave differently in experiments than in the real world, but to argue that the deviation from behavior from the actual economy is more significant in experiments than in formal models with abstract functions is hardly convincing (Schettkat 2010, 2012).

The axiomatic approach is attractive because it allows for a clear, logical structure with deduced precise results. However, the warning not to overinterpret the results of empirical analysis is quickly forgotten when the results of theoretical studies are interpreted. All real-world institutions look second best compared to the perfect market model, but its numerous conditions are never fulfilled. Nevertheless, observed deviations from the perfect market model are often described as "imperfections" or "anomalies." Still, it is the perfect market model which cannot be reconciled with actual economic behavior. "Anomalies" are actually the rule (Krueger 2018). Assuming that unfettered markets will automatically steer the economy to maximum welfare—the optimum, full employment—government interventions and regulations can only disturb the smooth market process. This hypothesis dominates neoclassical economic thinking and beyond and is well expressed in Reagan's "the state is the problem, not the solution." With the natural rate hypothesis, utility-maximizing unemployment and unique equilibrium were back, and the private sector was the efficiency machine only disturbed by public policy. Markets "know" the best and choose the most efficient. Still, the ingredients of the symbols of modern technology—the internet and the iPhone—are based on public research and investment (Mazzucato 2013).

References

Abel, B., Bernanke, B., Croushore, D. (2010). *Macroeconomics*. New York: Pearson.

Abernathy, W., Utterback, J. (1978). Patterns of industrial innovation. *Technology Review*, 80, June–July 1978.

Ainslie, G. (1991). Deviation of "rational" economic behavior from hyperbolic discount curves. *American Economic Review*, 81(2), 334–340.

Akerlof, G. (1982). Labor contracts as partial gift exchange. *Quarterly Journal of Economics*, 97, 543–569.

Akerlof, G. (2002). Behavioral macroeconomics and macroeconomic behavior. *American Economic Review*, 92(3), 411–433.

Akerlof, G. (2007). The missing motivation in macroeconomics. *American Economic Review*, 97(1), 5–36.

Akerlof, G., Kranton, R. (2011). *Identity economics: How our identities shape our work, wages, and well-being*. Princeton: Princeton University Press.

Akerlof, G., Shiller, R. (2009). *Animal Spirits: How Human Psychology Drives the Economy, and Why It Matters for Global Capitalism*. Princeton: Princeton University Press.

Akerlof, G., Shiller, R. J. (2015). *Phishing for Phools*. Princeton: Princeton University Press.

Akerlof, G., Yellen, J. (eds.) (1986). *Efficiency Wage Models of the Labor Market*. Cambridge: Cambridge University Press.

Akerlof, G., Yellen, J. (1987). Rational models of irrational behavior. *American Economic Review*, 77(2), 137–142.

Albin, P. (1998). *Barriers and Bounds to Rationality*. Princeton: Princeton University Press.

Alchian, A. (1953). The meaning of utility measurement. *American Economic Review*, 43, 26–50.

Aliber, R., Kindleberger, C. P. (2015). *Manias, Panics, and Crashes: A History of Financial Crises* (p. 256). Basingstoke: Palgrave Macmillan. (First edition: Kindleberger 1978.)

Allais, M. (1953). L'extension des théories de l'équilibre économique général et du rendement social au cas du risque. *Econometrica*, 503–546.

Allais, M. (1998). Allais paradox. In: Eatwell, J., Milgate, M., Newman, P. (eds.), *The New Palgrave. A Dictionary of Economics*. London: Macmillan Press, 80–82.

Appelbaum, E., Schettkat, R. (1995). Employment and productivity in industrialized economies. *International Labour Review*, 134, 605.

Ariely, D. (2008). *Predictably Irrational*. London: Harper Collins.

Arrow, K. (1959). Towards a theory of price adjustment. In: Ambramowitz, M. (ed.), *The Allocation of Economics Resources*. Stanford: Stanford University Press, 41–51.

Arrow, K. (1962). The economic implications of learning by doing. *The Review of Economic Studies*, 29(3, June), 155–173.

Arrow, K. J. (1978). The future and the present in economic life. *Economic Inquiry*, 16(2), 157–169.

Arrow, K. J. (1986). Rationality of self and others in an economic system. In: Hogarth, R., Reder, M. (eds.), *Rational Choice, The Contrast Between Economics and Psychology*. Chicago: University of Chicago Press, 201–216.

Arrow, K., Debreu, G. (1954). Existence of an equilibrium for a competitive economy. *Econometrica*, 22(3), 265–290.

Arthur, W. B. (1994a). *Increasing Returns and Path Dependence in the Economy*. Ann Arbor: University of Michigan Press.

Arthur, W. B. (1994b). Inductive reasoning and bounded rationality. *American Economic Review*, 84(2), 406–411. Papers and Proceedings of the Hundred and Sixth Annual Meeting of the American Economic Association (May).

Ashraf, N., Camerer, C. F., Loewenstein, G. (2005). Adam Smith, behavioral economist. *Journal of Economic Perspectives*, 19(3), 131–145.

Ball, L. (2009). Hysteresis in unemployment: Old and new evidence. *NBER Working Paper* No. 14818.

Ball, L., Mankiw, G. (1992). Relative-price changes as aggregate supply shocks. *NBER Working Paper* No. 4168.

Ball, L., Romer, D. (1990). Real rigidities and the non-neutrality of money. *Review of Economic Studies*, 57, 183–203.

Barens, I. (2011). 'Animal spirits' in John Maynard Keynes' general theory of employment, interest and money. Some short and sceptical remarks. *Darmstadt Discussion Papers in Economics*, No. 201.

Barnett, V. (2017). Keynes, animal spirits, and instinct: Reason plus intuition is better than rational. *Journal of the History of Economic Thought*, 39(3), 381–399.

Barr, N. (2001). *The Welfare State as Piggy Bank: Information, Risk, Uncertainty, and the Role of the State*. Oxford: Oxford University Press.

Baxter, J. (1988). *Social and Psychological Foundations of Economic Analysis* (Vol. 4). London: Harvester Wheatsheaf.

Becker, G. (1965). A theory of the allocation of time. *The Economic Journal*, 493–517.

Becker, G. (1993a). Nobel Lecture: the economic way of looking at behavior. *Journal of Political Economy*, 101(3), 385–409.

Becker, G. (1993b). *A Treatise on the Family*. Cambridge: Harvard University Press.

Bell, L., Freeman, R. (1985). Does a flexible industry wage structure increase employment?: The US experience. *NBER Working Paper* No. 1604.

Berczi, A. (1979). Chamberlin's experimental markets revisited: A computerized journey. *American Journal of Economics and Sociology*, 38(2), 197–206.

Berg, N., Gigerenzer, G. (2010). As-if behavioral economics: Neoclassical economics in disguise? *History of Economic Ideas*, 18(1), 1000–1033.

Bernanke, B. (2015). *The Courage to Act*. New York: Norton.
Bernanke, B., Gertler, M. (1995). Inside the black box: The credit channel of monetary policy transmission. *Journal or Economic Perspectives*, 9(4), 27–48.
Bernanke, B., Mihov, I. (1998). The liquidity effect and long-run neutrality. *NBER Working Paper* No. 6608.
Bernanke, B., Gertler, M., Watson, M. (1997). Systematic monetary policy and the effects of oil price shocks. *Brookings Papers on Economic Activity*, 28(1), 91–157.
Bernoulli, D. (1738). Specimen Theoriae Novae de Mensura Sortis, Imperial Academy of Sciences in Petersburg, vol V, pp. 175–192.Translation into English by Sommer, L. (1954). Exposition of a new theory on the measurement of risk. *Econometrica*, 22.s, 23–36.
Beshears, J, Choi, J., Laibson, D., Madrian, B. (2008). How are preferences revealed? *Journal of Public Economics*, 92(8–9), 1787–1794.
Bewley, T. F. (1995). A depressed labor market as explained by participants. *American Economic Review*, 85(2), 250–254.
Bewley, T. F. (1999). *Why Wages Don't Fall During a Recession*. Cambridge: Harvard University Press.
Blanchard, O. (1997). *Macroeconomics*. New Jersey: Prentice Hall.
Blanchard, O. (2000). *Macroeconomics*. New York: Pearson.
Blanchard, O., Wolfers, J. (2000). The role of shocks and institutions in the rise of European unemployment: The aggregate evidence. *The Economic Journal*, 110(462), C1–C33.
Blinder, A. S. (1979). *Economic Policy and the Great Stagflation*. New York: Academic Press.
Blinder, A. S. (1988). The fall and rise of Keynesian economics. *Economic Record*, 64(4), 278–294.
Blinder, A. S. (1990). Learning by asking those who are doing. *Eastern Economic Journal*, 16(4), 297–306.
Blinder, A. S. (1991). Why are prices sticky? Preliminary results from an interview study. *NBER Working Paper* No. w3646.
Blinder, A., Reis, R. (2005). *Understanding the Greenspan standard*. Princeton University, Center for Economic Policy Studies.
Blinder, A., Solow, R. (1973). Does fiscal policy matter? *Journal of Public Economics*, 2, 319–337.
Blinder, A. S, Canetti, E. R. D., Lebow, D. E., Rudd, J. B. (1998). *Asking about Prices*. New York: Russel Sage Foundation.
Bracha, A., Gneezy, U., Loewenstein, G. (2015). Relative pay and labor supply. *Journal of Labor Economics*, 33, 297–315.
Brainard, W., Perry, G. (2001). Making policy in a changing world. *Cowles Foundation Paper* No. 1011. New Haven, Yale University.
Burgess, S. (1993). A model of competition between unemployed and employed job searchers: An application to the unemployment outflow rate in Britain. *The Economic Journal*, 103(420), 1190–1204.
Caldwell, B. (1980). A critique of Friedman's methodological instrumentalism. *Southern Economic Journal*, 366–374.

Calvo, G. (1983). Staggered prices in a utility-maximizing framework. *Journal of Monetary Economics*, 12, 383–398.

Camerer, C., Loewenstein, G. (2004). Behavioral economics: Past, present, future. In: Camerer, C. F., Loewenstein, G., Rabin, M. (eds.), *Advances in Behavioral Economics*. Princeton: Princeton University Press, 3–52.

Camerer, C., Babcock, L., Loewenstein, G., Thaler, R. (1997). Labor supply of New York City cabdrivers: One day at a time. *The Quarterly Journal of Economics*, 112(2), 407–441.

Card, D., Krueger, A. (1995). *Myth and Measurement: The New Economics of the Minimum Wage*. Princeton: Princeton University Press.

Card, D. Mas, A., Moretti, E., Saez, E. (2010). Inequality at work: The effect of peer salaries on jobs satisfaction. *NBER Working Paper* No. 16396.

Carlin, W., Soskice, D. (1990). *The Macroeconomics of Wage Bargain*. Oxford: Oxford University Press.

Carlin, W., Soskice, D. (2008). Reforms, macroeconomic policy and economic performance in Germany. In Schettkat, R., Langkau, J. (eds.), *Economic Policy Proposals for Germany and Europe*. London and New York: Routledge Taylor & Francis, 72–118.

Chamberlin, E. (1948). An experimental imperfect market. *Journal of Political Economy*, 56(2), 95–108.

Chick, V. (2016). On microfoundations and Keynes' economics. *Review of Political Economy*, 28(1), 99–112.

Clark, A. E. (1999). Are wages habit-forming? Evidence from micro data. *Journal of Economic Behavior & Organization*, 39(2), 179–200.

Clark, A. E., Oswald, A. J. (1996). Satisfaction and comparison of income. *Journal of Public Economics*, 61(3), 359–381.

Clark, A. E., Frijters, P., Shields, M. A. (2008). Relative income, happiness, and utility: An explanation for the Easterlin Paradox and other puzzles. *Journal of Economic Literature*, 46(1), 95–144.

Clark, K., Summers, L. (1982). Labour force participation: Timing and persistence. *The Review of Economic Studies*, 49(5), 825–844.

Coase, R. (1937). The nature of the firm. Reprinted from: *Economica*, 4, 386–405.

Cohen, J. (2005). The vulcanization of the human brain: A neural perspective on interactions between cognition and emotion. *Journal of Economic Perspectives*, 19(4), 3–24.

Conlisk, J. (1996). Why bounded rationality?, *Journal of Economic Literature*, XXXIV, 669–700.

Council of Economic Advisers (1962). *Annual Report 1962*. U.S. G.A.O.

Damásio, A. (1994). *Descartes' Error: Emotion, Reason and the Human Brain*. London: Picador.

David, P. (1990). The dynamo and the computer: An historical perspective on the modern productivity paradox. *American Economic Review*, 80(2), 355–361.

de Grauwe, P. (2011). Animal spirits and monetary policy. *Economic Theory*, 47(2–3), 423–457.

de Grauwe, P. (2012). Booms and busts in economic activity: A behavioral explanation. *Journal of Economic Behavior & Organization*, 83(3), 484–501.

de Grauwe, P., Costa Storti, C. (2008). Monetary policy and the real economy. In: Schettkat, R., Langkau, J. (eds.), *Economic Policy Proposals for Germany and Europe*. London and New York: Routledge Taylor & Francis, 29–53.

de Grauwe, P., Polan, M. (2005). Is inflation always and everywhere a monetary phenomenon? *Scandinavian Journal of Economics*, 107(2), 239–259.

Diamond, P. (2010). Unemployment, vacancies, wages. Prize Lecture, Stockholm, December 8.

Dohmen, T., Falk, A., Fliessbach, K., Sunde, U., Weber, B. (2011). Relative versus absolute income, joy of winning, and gender: Brain imaging evidence. *Journal of Public Economics*, 95(3):279–285.

Domar, E. (1946). Capital expansion, rate of growth, and employment. *Econometrica*, 14(2), 137–147.

Dow, S. (2012). Uncertainty about uncertainty. In: Dow, S. (ed.), *Foundations for New Economic Thinking, A Collection of Essays*. London: Palgrave Macmillan, 72–82.

Drakopoulos, S. (2011). The neglect of comparison income: A historical perspective. *The European Journal of the History of Economic Thought*, 18(3), 441–464.

Duesenberry, J. (1949). *Income, Saving, and the Theory of Consumer Behavior*. Cambridge: Harvard University Press.

Duflo, E., Banerjee, A. (2019). Economic incentives don't always do what we want them to. *New York Times*, October 26.

Dunlop, J. G. (1938). The movement of real and money wages. *Economic Journal*, 48, 413–433.

Einhorn, H., Hogarth, R. (1986). Decision making under ambiguity. *Journal of Business*, 59(4), S225–S250.

Eisner, R. (1994). *The Misunderstood Economy: What Counts and How to Count It*. Cambridge: Harvard Business School Press.

Eisner, R. (1997). A new view of the NAIRU. In Davidson, P., Kregel, J. (eds.), *Improving the Global Economy: Keynesian and the Growth in Output and Employment*. Cheltenham, UK and Lyme, NH, USA: Edward Elgar Publishing, 196–230.

Ellsberg, D. (1961). Risk, ambiguity, and the savage axioms. *The Quarterly Journal of Economics*, 643–669.

Ellsberg, D. (2001). *Risk, Ambiguity, Decision*. New York: Garland.

Elsner, W. (2012). *Microeconomics of Interactive Economies*. Cheltenham, UK and Northampton, MA, USA: Edward Elgar Publishing.

Falk, A.; Fehr, E., Zehnder, C. (2006). Fairness perceptions and reservation wages: The behavioral effects of minimum wage laws. *The Quarterly Journal of Economics*, 121(4), 1347–1381.

Feduzi, A. (2007). On the relationship between Keynes' conception of evidential weight and the Ellsberg paradox. *Journal of Economic Psychology*, 28(5), 545–565.

Fehr, E., Schmidt, K. (1999). A theory of fairness, competition and cooperation. *Quarterly Journal of Economics*, 114, 817–868.

Fishlow, A. (1965). *American Railroads and the Transformation of the American Economy*. Cambridge: Harvard University Press.

Flanagan, R., Strauss, G., Ulman, L. (1974). Worker discontent and work place behavior. *Industrial Relations: A Journal of Economy and Society*, 13(2), 101–123.

Fliessbach, K. et al. (2007). Social comparison affects reward-related brain activity in the human ventral striatum. *Science*, 318(5854), 1305–1308.

Flinn, C. (2010). *The Minimum Wage and Labor Market Outcomes*. Cambridge: MIT Press.

Frank, R. (1985). *Choosing the Right Pond: Human Behavior and the Quest for Status*. Oxford: Oxford University Press.

Frank, R. (1999). *Luxury Fever: Weighing the Cost of Excess* (p. 78). Princeton: Princeton University Press.

Frank, R. (2008). Lessons from behavioral economics: Interview with Robert Frank. *Challenge*, 51(3), 80–92.

Freeman, C., Soete, L. (1997). *The Economics of Industrial Innovation*. London and Washington. Pinter.

Freeman, R. (1978). Job satisfaction as an economic variable. *American Economic Review*, 68(2), 135–141. Papers and Proceedings.

Freeman, R. (2005). Labour market institutions without blinders: The debate over flexibility and labour market performance. *International Economic Journal*, 19(2), 129–145.

Freeman, R. B. (2008). Why do we work more than Keynes expected?. In: Pechi, L., Piga, G. (eds.), *Revisiting Keynes: Economics Perspectives for our Grandchildren*. Cambridge: MIT Press, 136–178.

Freeman, R., Schettkat, R. (2005). Marketization of household production and the EU–US gap in work. *Economic Policy*, 20(41), 6–50.

Frey, B., Stutzer, A. (2002). *Happiness & Economics*. Princeton: Princeton University Press.

Friedman, B. (1979). Optimal expectations and the extreme information assumptions of 'rational expectations' macromodels. *Journal of Monetary Economics*, 5(1), 23–41.

Friedman, B. (1984). Lessons from the 1979–1982 monetary policy experiment. *NBER Working Paper* No. 1272.

Friedman, M. (1953). *Essays in Positive Economics*. Chicago: University of Chicago Press.

Friedman, M. (1956). The quantity theory of money: A restatement, In: Friedman, M. (ed.), *Studies in the Quantity Theory of Money*. Chicago: University of Chicago Press, 1–21.

Friedman, M. (1957). The permanent income hypothesis. In *A Theory of the Consumption Function*. Princeton: Princeton University Press, 20–37.

Friedman, M. (1968). The role of monetary policy. *American Economic Review*, 58(1), 1–17.

Friedman, M. (1975). Perspectives on inflation. *Newsweek*, June 24, 73.

Friedman, M. (1976). Inflation and unemployment. *Nobel Memorial Lecture*, December 13, 1976.

Friedman, M. (2006). Tradeoffs in monetary policy. *Paper prepared for David Laidler's Festschrift*.

Friedman, M., Friedman, R. (1990). *Free to Choose: A Personal Statement*. Boston: Houghton Mifflin Harcourt.

Friedman, M., Savage, L. (1948). The utility analysis of choices involving risk. *Journal of Political Economy*, 56, 279–304.

Friedman, M., Savage, L. (1952). The expected utility hypothesis and measurability of utility. *The Journal of Political Economy*, December, 463–474.

Frisch, R. (1953). Editors comment on Allais. *Econometrica*, 269.

Fröba, S., Wassermannm A. (2007). *Die bedeutendsten Mathematiker*, Wiesbaden: Marix Verlag.

Frydman, R., Goldberg, M. D. (2011). *Beyond Mechanical Markets: Asset Price Swings, Risk, and the Role of the State*. Princeton: Princeton University Press.

Gagnon, J. (2017). There is no inflation puzzle. Peterson Institute for International Economics, Washington.

Galbraith, J. (1987). *Economics in Perspective, A Critical History*. Boston: Houghton Mifflin.

Gigerenzer, G. (2001). Decision making: Nonrational theories. In: Wright, J. (ed.) *International Encyclopedia of the Social and Behavioral Sciences*. Elsevier Science, 3304–3309.

Gigerenzer, G. (2017). How do smart people make smart decisions?, YouTube.

Gigerenzer, G., Selten, R. (2001). Rethinking rationality. In: Gigerenzer, G., Selten, R. (eds.), *Bounded Rationality: The Adaptive Toolbox*. Cambridge: MIT Press, 1–12.

Gordon, R. (2013). The Phillips curve is alive and well: Inflation and the NAIRU during the slow recovery. *NBER Working Paper* No. w19390.

Gorter C., Schettkat, R. (2009). On musical chairs and matching models: Do employed job seekers crowd-out the unemployed? *Future of Economic Science*, 325.

Greenwald, B., Stiglitz, J. (1989). Toward a theory of rigidities. *American Economic Review*, 79(May), 364–369.

Güth, W. (2008). (Non-) behavioral economics: A programmatic assessment. *Journal of Psychology*, 216, 244–253.

Hagemann, H. (2019). Economic possibilities for our grandchildren. In: Dimand, R., Hagemann, H. (eds.) *Elgar Companion to John Maynard Keynes*. Cheltenham, UK and Northampton, MA, USA: Edward Elgar Publishing, 162–167.

Hahn, F. (1977). Keynesian economics and general equilibrium theory: Reflections on some current debates. In: Harcourt, G. (ed.), *Microeconomic Foundations of Macroeconomics*. London: Palgrave Macmillan, 25–40.

Hahn, F. (1980). General equilibrium theory. *The Public Interest*, Fall, 123–138.

Hahn, F., Solow, R. (1986). Is wage flexibility a good thing? In: Beckerman, W. (ed.), *Wage Rigidity and Unemployment*. London: Duckworth, 1–19.

Hamilton, J. D. (2011). Historical oil shocks. *NBER Working Paper* No.16790.

Hansen, A. (1936). Mr. Keynes on underemployment equilibrium. *Journal of Political Economy*, 44(5), 667–686.

Hansen, A. (1953). *A Guide to Keynes*. New York: McGraw-Hill.

Harrod, R. (1937). Mr. Keynes and traditional theory. *Econometrica*, 5(1), 74–86.

Harrod, R. (1939). An essay in dynamic theory. *The Economic Journal*, 49(193), 14–33.

Hassink, W. H., Schettkat, R. (2003). Price discrimination between EU regions. *Tijdschrift Voor Economische en Sociale Geografie*, 94(2), 258–264.

Hicks, J. (1936). Keynes' Theory of Employment, *The Economic Journal*, 46, No. 182, 238-253.

Hicks, J. (1937). Mr. Keynes and the "classics". A suggested interpretation. *Econometrica*, 5, 147–159.

Hicks, J. (1980). IS-LM: An explanation. *Journal of Post Keynesian Economics*, 3(2), 139–154.

Hirsch, F. (1976). *Social Limits to Growth*. Cambridge: Harvard University Press.

Hirschman, A. O. (1992). *Rival Views of Market Society*. Cambridge: Harvard University Press.

Hirshleifer, J., Riley, J. (1992). *The Analytics of Uncertainty and Information*. Cambridge: Cambridge University Press.

Horn, G., Logeay, C., Tober, S. (2007). Methodological issues of medium-term macroeconomic projections – the case of potential output. *IMK Study*, No.4/2007.

Howitt, P. (1986). The Keynesian recovery. *Canadian Journal of Economics*, 626–641.

Hsu, M., Bhatt, M, Adolphs, R., Tranel, D., Camerer, C. (2005). Neural systems responding to degrees of uncertainty in human decision-making. *Science*, 310, 1680–1683.

Ironmonger, D. (2000). Household production and the household economy. Research Paper, Department of Economics, University of Melbourne.

Issing, O. (2000). The monetary policy of the European Central Bank: Strategy and implementation. *CESifo Forum*.

Jackson, M., Yariv, L. (2020). The Non-Existence of Representative Agents. Manuscript, Stanford University, Santa Fe Institute, Princeton University.

Jäncke, L. (2015). *Ist das Hirn vernüftig? Erkenntnise eines Neuropsychologen*. Bern: hogrefe.

Johnson, H. (1971). The Keynesian revolution and the monetarist counter-revolution. *American Economic Review*, 1–14.

Kahn, R. (1976). Unemployment as seen by the Keynesians. In: Worsick, G. (ed.), *The Concept and Measurement of Involuntary Unemployment*. London: HarperCollins, 19–34.

Kahneman, D. (2002). Maps of bounded rationality: A perspective on intuitive judgment and choice. *Prize Lecture*, December 8, pp. 449–489.

Kahneman, D. (2011). *Thinking Fast and Slow*. London: Penguin Books.

Kahneman, D., Thaler, R. H. (2006). Anomalies: Utility maximization and experienced utility. *Journal of Economic Perspectives*, 20(1), 221–234.

Kahneman D., Tversky, A. (1972). Subjective probability: A judgment of representativeness. *Cognitive Psychology*, 3, 430–454.

Kahneman, D., Tversky, A. (1979). Prospect theory: An analysis of decision under risk. *Econometrica*, 47(2), 263–291.

Kahneman D., Tversky, A. (1984). Choices, values, and frames. *American Psychologist*, 34. Reprinted in Kahneman, D. (2011). *Thinking Fast and Slow*. London: Penguin, 433–448.

Kahneman, D., Tversky, A. (eds.) (2000). *Choices, Values, and Frames*. Cambridge: Russell Sage Foundation, Cambridge University Press.

Kahneman, D., Knetsch, J., Thaler, R. (1986). Fairness as a constraint on profit seeking: Entitlements in the market. *American Economic Review*, 76(4), 728–741.

Kahneman, D., Knetsch, J., Thaler, R. (1991). Anomalies: The endowment effect, loss aversion, and status quo bias. *Journal of Economic Perspectives*, 5(1), 193–206.

Kaldor, N. (1934). A classificatory note on the determinateness of equilibrium. *The Review of Economic Studies*, 1(2), 122–136.

Kaldor, N. (1972). The irrelevance of equilibrium economics. *The Economic Journal*, 82, 1237–1255.

Kalecki, M. (1971). *Selected Essays on the Dynamics of the Capitalist Economy 1933–1970*. Cambridge: Cambridge University Press.

Kalmbach, P. (1985). Lohnhöhe und Beschäftigung: Ein Evergreen der wirtschaftspolitischen Debatte. *Wirtschaftsdienst*, 65, 370–376.

Katz, L., Krueger, A. (1999). The high-pressure U.S. labor market of the 1990s. *Brookings Papers on Economic Activity*, 1999:1.

Keynes, J. M. (1921). *A Treatise on Probability*. London: Macmillan.

Keynes, J. M. (1930). The economic possibilities for our grandchildren. In *Essays in Persuasion*, New York: Harcourt Brace, 1932, 358–373.

Keynes, J. (1936). *The General Theory of Employment, Interest and Money*. London: Macmillan.

Keynes, J. (1937). The general theory of employment. *Quarterly Journal of Economics*, 51(2), 209–223.

Keynes, J. (1939). Relative movement of real wages and output. *Economic Journal*, 193, 34–51. Reprinted in Keynes, J. (1981). *The General Theory of Employment, Interest and Money*. London/Basingstoke: Macmillan Press.

Kilian, L. (2008). Exogenous oil supply shocks: How big are they and how much do they matter for the U.S. economy?. *The Review of Economics and Statistics*, 90(2), 216–240.

Killingsworth, M.R. (1983). *Labor Supply*. Cambridge/London: Cambridge University Press.

Kindleberger, C. P. (1978). *Manias, Panics, and Crashes: A History of Financial Crises*. New York: Basic Books.

Kirman, A. P. (1992). Whom or what does the representative individual represent? *Journal of Economic Perspectives*, 6(2), 117–136.

Klein, L. (1944). *The Keynesian Revolution*. Dissertation at MIT, supervisor P. Samuelson, Department of Economics, published 1947 as: *The Keynesian Revolution*. Macmillan, London 1947.

Knight, F.H. (1921). *Risk, Uncertainty, and Profit*. Boston: Houghton Mifflin.

Komlos, J. (2014). Behavioral indifference curves. *NBER Working Paper* No. 20240.

Koppl, R. (1991). Retrospectives: Animal spirits. *Journal of Economic Perspectives*, 5(3), 203–210.

Kornai, J. (1971). *Anti-Equilibrium*. Amsterdam: North-Holland.

Kromphardt, J. (1985). Die Phillipskurve bei informierter Erwartungsbildung: Replik. *Zeitschrift für Wirtschafts- und Sozialwissenschaften*, 105(5), 631–644.

Kromphardt, J. (2013). *Die Größten Ökonomen: John Maynard Keynes*. Munich: UVK-Verlagsgesellschaft, Konstanz.

Kromphardt, J., Logeay, C. (2011). Flattening of the Phillips curve: Estimations and consequences for economic policy. *Intervention*, 8(1), 43–67.

Krueger, A. (2018). Luncheon Address: Reflections on dwindling worker bargaining power and monetary policy, Jackson Hole Economic Policy Symposium, Changing Market Structures and Implications for Monetary Policy, The Federal Reserve Bank of Kansas City.

Krueger, A., Ashenfelter, O. (2018). Theory and evidence on employer collusion in the franchise sector. *NBER Working Paper* No. 24831.

Krueger, A., Mas, A. (2003). Strikes, scabs and tread separations: Labor strife and the production of defective Bridgestone/Firestone Tires. *NBER Working Paper* No. 9524.

Krueger, A. B., Summers, L. H. (1987). Reflections on the inter-industry wage structure. In Lang, K., Leonard, J. S. (eds.), *Unemployment and the Structure of Labor Markets*. London: Blackwell, 17–47.

Krueger, A. B., Summers, L. H. (1988). Efficiency wages and the inter-industry wage structure. *Econometrica: Journal of the Econometric Society*, 259–293.

Krugman, P. (2021). Wonking out: A very Austrian pandemic. *New York Times*, September 3.

Kuhn, T. S. (1970). *The Structure of Scientific Revolutions*, 2nd edition. Chicago: University of Chicago Press.

Kurz, H. (2018). *Das Gespenst säkularer Stagnation*. Marburg: metropois.

Lam, M-Y. (2016). *Review of learning*. Master Thesis, University of Wuppertal.

Layard, R. (2005). *Happiness*. New York: Penguin.

Layard, R., Nickell, S., Jackman, R. (1991). *Unemployment: Macroeconomic Performance and the Labour Market*. Oxford: Oxford University Press.

Leibenstein, H. (1976). *Beyond Economic Man*. Cambridge: Harvard University Press.

Leijonhufvud, A. (1967). Keynes and Keynesians: A suggested interpretation. *American Economic Review*, 57, 401–10.

Leijonhufvud, A. (1973). Life among the Econ. *Economic Inquiry*, 11(3), 327–337.

Lekachman, R. (ed.) (1964). *Keynes' General Theory: Reports of Three Decades*. New York: St. Martin's.

Leontief, W. (1934). Verzögerte Angebotsanpassung und partielles Gleichgewicht. *Zeitschrift für Nationalökonomie*, 5(5), 670–676.

Leontief, W. (1936). The fundamental assumptions of Mr. Keynes' monetary theory of unemployment. *The Quarterly Journal of Economics*, 51(I), 192–197.

Leontief, W. (1947). Postulates: Keynes' general theory and the classics. In: Harris, S. (ed.) *The NEW Economics*. New York: Knopf, 232–242. Reprinted in Lekachman (1964). *Keynes' General Theory: Reports of Three Decades*. New York: St. Martin's.

Leontief, W. (1971). Theoretical assumptions and nonobserved facts. *American Economic Review*, 1–7.

Lerner, A. (1936). Mr Keynes' "General Theory of Employment, Interest and Money". *International Labour Review*. International Labour Organization (ILO), pp. 36–46. Reprinted in Lekachman (1964). *Keynes' General Theory: Reports of Three Decades*. New York: St. Martin's, 203–222.

Lerner, J., Li, Y., Valdeso, P., Kassam, K. (2015). Emotions and decision making, *Annual Review of Psychology*, 799–823.

Loewenstein, G., Sicherman, N. (1991). Do workers prefer increasing wage profiles? *Journal of Labor Economics*, 9(1), 67–84.

Loewenstein, G., Rick, S., Cohen, J. (2008). Neuroeconomics. *Annual Review of Psychology*, January, 647–674.

Lucas, R. (1972). Expectations and the neutrality of money. *Journal of Economic Theory*, 4, 103–124.

Lucas, R. (1986). Adaptive behavior and economic theory. In: Hogarth, R., Reder, M. (eds.), *Rational Choice, The Contrast Between Economics and Psychology*. Chicago: University of Chicago Press, 217–242.

Lucas, R., Sargent, T. (1978). After the Phillips curve: Persistence of high inflation and high unemployment. In *FRBB, Conference Series*, No. 19, pp. 49–68.

Lucas, R., Sargent, T. (1979). After Keynesian macroeconomics. *Federal Reserve Bank of Minneapolis Quarterly Review*, 3(2), 1–16.

Machina, M. (1987). Choice under uncertainty: Problems solved and unsolved. *Journal of Economic Perspectives*, 1(1), 121–154.

Mankiw, G. (1985). Small menu costs and large business cycles: A macroeconomic model of monopoly. *The Quarterly Journal of Economics*, 100(2), 529–537.

Mankiw, G. (2000). The inexorable and mysterious tradeoff between inflation and unemployment. *NBER Working Paper* No. 7884.

Manning, A. (2003). *Monopsony in Motion: Imperfect Competition in Labor Markets*. Princeton: Princeton University Press.

Marglin, S. (2018). The General Theory after 80 years. In: Hagemann, H., Kromphardt, J., Martenbauer M. (eds.), *Keynes, Geld und Finanzen*. Schriften der Keynes-Gesellschaft, Band 11, Marburg: Metropolis, 27–56.

Marschak, J. (1950). Rational behavior, uncertain prospects, and measurable utility. *Econometrica*, 18(2), 111–141.

Marshall, A. (1890). *Principles of Economics*. Reprinted eighth edition, 1979. London/Basingstoke: Macmillan Press.

Martinez, I., Saez, E., Siegenthaler, M. (2018). Intertemporal labor supply substitution? Evidence from the Swiss income tax holidays. *NBER Working Paper* No. 24634.

Mazzucato, M. (2013). *The Entrepreneurial State: Debunking Public vs. Private Myths in Risk and Innovation*. London: Anthem Press.

Medoff, J. L., Abraham, K. G. (1980). Experience, performance, and earnings. *The Quarterly Journal of Economics*, 95(4), 703–736.

Medoff, J. L., Abraham, K. G. (1981). Are those paid more really more productive? The case of experience. *Journal of Human Resources*, 186–216.

Minsky, H. P. (1977). The financial instability hypothesis: An interpretation of Keynes and an alternative to "standard" theory. *Challenge*, 20(1), 20–27.

Minsky, H. P. (1992). The financial instability hypothesis. Working Paper No. 74, May 1992, papers.ssrn.com.

Mishkin, F. (2010). *The Economics of Money, Banking & Financial Markets*. New York: Pearson.

Muth, J. (1961). Rational expectations and the theory of price movements. *Econometrica*, 29(3), 315–335.

Myrdal, G. (1957). *Economic Theory and Underdeveloped Regions*. London: University Paperbacks, Methuen.

Nakamura, E., Steinsson, J., Sun, P., Villar, D. (2018). The elusive costs of inflation: Price dispersion during the U.S. great inflation. *Quarterly Journal of Economics*, 133, 1933–1980.

Nelson, R. R., Winter, S. G. (1982). *An Evolutionary Theory of Economic Change*. Cambridge: The Belknap Press of Harvard University Press.

Neumark, D., Postlewaite, A. (1998). Relative income concerns and the rise in married women's employment. *Journal of Public Economics*, 70(1), 157–183.

Nobel Prize Committee, Prize in Economic Science 1988, https://www.nobelprize.org/prizes/economic-sciences/1988/allais/facts/.

Nobel Prize Committee, Prize in Economic Science 1980, https://www.nobelprize.org/prizes/economic-sciences/1980/klein/facts/.

OECD (1994). *The OECD Jobs Study*. Paris: OECD.

Okun, A. (1981). *Prices and Quantities, A Macroeconomic Analysis*. Cambridge: Brookings Institution Press.

Pasinetti, L. (2007). *Keynes and the Cambridge Keynesians: A "Revolution in Economics" to be Accomplished*. Cambridge: Cambridge University Press.

Patinkin, D. (1948). Price flexibility and full employment. *American Economic Review*, 38(4), 543–564.

Pesendorfer, W. (2006). *Behavioral Economics Comes to Age*. Manuscript. Princeton: Princeton University.

Peters, O. (2019). The ergodicity problem in economics. *Nature Physics*, 15, 1216–1221. https://doi.org/10.1038/s41567-019-0732-0.

Peters, O., Gell-Mann, M. (2016). Evaluating gambles using dynamics. *Chaos*, 26, https://doi.org/10.1063/1.4940236.

PEW Research Center (2006). Things we can't live without: The list has grown in the past decade. *Report*. December 14. Washington D.C.

Phelps, E. S. (1967). Phillips curves, expectations of inflation and optimal unemployment over time. *Economica*, 254–281.

Phelps, E. S. (1968). Money-wage dynamics and labor-market equilibrium. *Journal of Political Economy*, 76(4, Part 2), 678–711.

Phelps, E. S. (1970). Introduction: The new microeconomics in employment and inflation theory. In Phelps, E. S. et al. (eds.), *Microeconomic Foundations of Employment and Inflation Theory*. New York: Norton. 1–23.

Phillips, A. W. (1958). The relation between unemployment and the rate of change of money wage rates in the UK, 1861–1957. *Economica*, 22, 283–299.

Popper, K. (1959). *The Logic of Scientific Discovery*. London: Routledge.
Ramsey, F. (1926). Truth and probability. In: Braithwaite, R. (ed.), *The Foundations of Mathematics and other Logical Essays*. Patterson: Littlefield, Adams & Co., 156–203.
Rangel, B., Wibral, M., Falk, A. (2009). The medial prefrontal cortex exhibits money illusion. *Proceedings of the National Academy of Science*, USA, 106(13), 5025–5028.
Riedl, A. (2009). Behavioral and experimental economics can inform public policy: Some thoughts. CESifo: Working Paper No. 2902.
Robertson, D. (1936). Some Notes on Mr. Keynes' General Theory of Employment, *Quarterly Journal of Economics*, Vol. 51, 169–191. Reprinted in Lekachman (1964). *Keynes' General Theory: Reports of Three Decades*. New York: St. Martin's, 235–253.
Robinson, J. (1962). *Economic Philosophy*. London, Penguin.
Romer, C., Romer, D. H. (1994). What ends recessions?. *NBER Macroeconomics Annual*, 9, 13–57.
Rosenberg, N. (1994). *Exploring the Black Box: Technology, Economics, and History*. Cambridge: Cambridge University Press.
Rothschild, K. W. (1981). *Einführung in die Ungleichgewichtstheorie*. Berlin and Heidelberg: Springer Verlag.
Rothschild, K. W. (1988). *Theorien der Arbeitslosigkeit*. München und Wien: Oldenbourg.
Rothschild, K. W. (1993). *Employment, Wages And Income Distribution: Critical Essays in Economics*. London: Routledge.
Russo, G., Gorter, C., Schettkat, R. (2001). Searching, hiring and labour market conditions. *Labour Economics*, 553–571.
Sakai, Y. (2018). Daniel Ellsberg on J.M. Keynes and F.H. Knight: Risk ambiguity and uncertainty. *Evolutionary and Institutional Economic Review*, 1–18.
Salter, W. (1960). *Productivity and Technical Change*, 2nd edition 1966. Cambridge: Cambridge University Press.
Samuelson, P. (1952). Probability, utility, and the independence axiom. *Econometrica*, 20, 670–678.
Samuelson, P. (1963). Discussion. *American Economic Review*, 53(2), Papers and Proceedings, 231–236.
Samuelson, P., Solow, R. (1960). Analytical aspects of anti-inflation policy. *American Economic Review*, 50(2), 177–194.
Samuelson, W., Zeckhauser, R. (1988). Status quo bias in decision making. *Journal of Risk and Uncertainty*, 1(1), 7–59.
Schelling, T. C. (1978). *Micromotives and Macrobehavior*. New York: W.W. Norton & Company.
Schettkat, R. (1992). *The Labor Market Dynamics of Economic Restructuring, The United States and Germany in Transition*. New York: Praeger Publishers.
Schettkat, R. (1993). Compensating differentials? Wage differentials and employment stability in the U.S. and the German economies. *The Journal of Economic Issues*, 27(March), 153–170.
Schettkat, R. (1994). Flexibility through labour mobility: A function of the macroeconomy. *Structural Change and Economic Dynamics*, 5(2), 383–392.

Schettkat, R. (1996a). Labor market flows over the business cycle: An asymmetric hiring cost explanation. *Journal of Theoretical and Institutional Economics*, 152(4), 641–653.

Schettkat, R. (1996b). The flow approach to labor market analysis: Introduction. In: Schettkat, R. (ed.), *The Flow Analysis of Labour Markets,* Schettkat. London: Routledge, 17–29.

Schettkat, R. (2010). Will only an earthquake shake up economics? *International Labour Review*, 149(2), 185–207.

Schettkat, R. (2012). Book Review: Flinn, C.: Minimum wages and labor market outcomes. *Journal of Economics*, 283–286.

Schettkat, R. (2018a). Revision or revolution? A note on behavioral vs. neoclassical economics. Discussion Paper, Schumpeter School of Economics.

Schettkat, R., Jovicic, S. (2017). Macroeconomic revolution on shaky grounds: Lucas/Sargent critique's inherent contradictions, *Working Paper May 2017*, Washington Center for Equitable Growth.

Schettkat, R., Sun, R. (2009). Monetary policy and European unemployment. *Oxford Review of Economic Policy*, 25(1), 94–108.

Schettkat, R., Yocarini, L. (2001). Education driving the rise in Dutch female employment explanations for the increase in part-time work and female employment in the Netherlands, contrasted with Germany. *IAW-Report 1/ 2003*, Institut für Angewandte Wirtschaftsforschung Tübingen, 27–66.

Schlicht, E. (1978). Labour turnover, wage structure, and natural unemployment. *Zeitschrift für die gesamte Staatswissenschaft*, 134, 337–346.

Schulmeister, S. (2018). *Der Weg Zur Prosperität*. Wals bei Salzburg: Ecowin.

Schumpeter, J. (1911). *Theorie der Wirtschaftlichen Entwicklung, Eine Untersuchung über Unternehmergewinn, Kapital, Kredit, Zins und den Konjunkutrzyklus*. Berlin: Duncker & Humblot.

Schumpeter, J. (1939). *Business Cycles: A Theoretical, Historical, and Statistical Analysis of the Capitalist Process*. New York/London, McGraw-Hill.

Schumpeter, J. (1948). Science and ideology. *American Economics Review*, 345–359.

Scitovsky, T. (1976). *The Joyless Economy: An Inquiry into Human Satisfaction and Consumer Dissatisfaction*. New York: Oxford University Press.

Selten, R. (1990). Evolution, learning, and economic behavior. *Games and Economic Behavior*, 3, 3–24.

Sen, A. K. (1977). Rational fools: A critique of the behavioral foundations of economic theory. *Philosophy and Public Affairs*, 4(6), 317–344.

Sent, E-M. (2004). Behavioral economics: How psychology made its (limited) way back into economics. *History of Political Economy*, 36(4), 735–760.

Shackle, G. L. S. (1958). *Time in Economics*. Amsterdam: North-Holland Publishing Company.

Shafir, E., Diamond, P., Tversky, A. (1997). Money illusion. *The Quarterly Journal of Economics*, 112(2), 341–374.

Shiller, R. (2021). Animal spirits and viral popular narratives. *Review of Keynesian Economics*, 9(4), 1–10.

Simon, H. (1955). A behavioral model of rational choice. *Quarterly Journal of Economics*, 69, 99–118.

Simon, H. (1963). Discussion. *American Economic Review*, 53(2), Papers and Proceedings, 229–231.

Simon, H. (1978). Rational decision-making in business organizations. *Lecture in Memory of Alfred Nobel*, December 8, 1978. Nobelprize.org. and in: *American Economic Review* (1979), vol. 69, 493–513.

Simon, H. (1982). *Models of Bounded Rationality: Behavioral Economics and Business Organization*, vol. 2. Cambridge: MIT Press.

Simon, H. (1986). Rationality in psychology and economics. In: Hogarth, R., Reder, M. (eds.), *Rational Choice, The Contrast between Economics and Psychology*. Chicago: University of Chicago Press, 25–40.

Skidelsky, R. (2003). *John Maynard Keynes 1883–1946, Economist, Philosopher, Statesman*. New York: Penguin.

Slovic, P., Tversky, A. (1974). Who accepts Savage's axiom? *Behavioral Science*, 19(6), 368–373.

Smith, A. (1759). 1790. *The theory of moral sentiments*.

Smith, A. (1776). *An Inquiry into the Nature and Causes of the Wealth of Nations*.

Smith, V. (2002a). Constructivist and ecological rationality in economics. Prize Lecture, Nobel Prize Committee.

Smith, V (2002b). Biographical. NobelPrize.org. Nobel Prize Outreach.

Solow, R. M. (1956). A contribution to the theory of economic growth. *The Quarterly Journal of Economics*, 70(1), 65–94.

Solow, R. M. (1974). The economics of resources or the resources of economics. *American Economic Review*, 64(2), 1–14.

Solow, R. (1978). Summary and evaluation. In *After the Phillips Curve: Persistence of High Inflation and High Unemployment*. Federal Reserve Bank of Boston Conference Series No. 19, pp. 49–72.

Solow, R. M. (1979). Another possible source of wage stickiness. *Journal of Macroeconomics*, 1, 79–82.

Solow, R. M. (1985). Unemployment: Getting the questions right. *Economica*, 53, S23–S34.

Solow, R. M. (1990). *The Labor Market as a Social Institution*. London: Blackwell.

Solow, R. (2000). Unemployment in the United States and in Europe. A contrast and the reasons. *CESifo Working Paper* Series No. 231.

Solow, R. (2008). Broadening the discussion of macroeconomic policy. In: Schettkat, R., Langkau, J. (eds.), *Economic Policy Proposals for Germany and Europe*. London and New York: Routledge Taylor & Francis Group, 20–28.

Spence, M. (1973). Job market signaling. *The Quarterly Journal of Economics*, 87(3), 355–374.

Starmer, C. (2004). Friedman's risky methodology. University of Nottingham Working Paper.

Stern, N. (2006). Stern Review: The economics of climate change.

Stigler, G. J. (1946). The economics of minimum wage legislation. *American Economic Review*, 36(3), 358–365.

Stigler, G., Becker, G. (1977). De Gustibus Non Est Disputandum. *American Economic Review*, 67(2, March), 76–90.

Stiglitz, J. (1986). *Economics of the Public Sector*. New York: W.W. Norton & Company.
Stiglitz, J. (2012). Lecture, Commonwealth Club San Francisco, California, June 12, FORA TV, YouTube.
Stock, J., Watson, M. (2019). Slack and Cyclically Sensitive Inflation, *NBER Working Paper* No. 25987.
Taleb, N. (2007). *The Black Swan, Impact of the Highly Improbable*. New York: Random House.
Tarshis, L. (1939). Changes in real and money wages. *Economic Journal*, 49, 150–154.
Taylor, J. (2000). Comment on Brainard, W., Perry, G. (2001). *Manuscript*. Stanford: Stanford University.
Thaler, R. H. (1981). Some empirical evidence on dynamic inconsistency. *Economic Letters*, 8(3), 201–207.
Thaler, R. H. (2015). *Misbehaving. The Making of Behavioral Economics*. New York: W.W. Norton & Company.
Thaler, R., Sunstein, C. (2008). *Nudge: The Gentle Power of Choice Architecture*. New Haven: Yale University Press.
Thurow, L. C. (1975). *Generating Inequality*. New York: Basic Books.
Tobin, J. (1972). Inflation and unemployment. *American Economic Review*, 62, 1–18.
Tobin, J. (1975). Keynesian models of recession and depression. *American Economic Review*, 65(2), 195–202.
Tobin, J. (1995). The natural rate as new classical macroeconomics. In: Cross, R. (ed.), *The Natural Rate of Unemployment*. Cambridge: Cambridge University Press, 32–42.
Tobin, J. (1997). Supply constraints on employment and output: NAIRU versus natural rate. Cowles Foundation Discussion Papers *1150*, Cowles Foundation for Research in Economics, Yale University.
Trevithick, J. A. (1976). Money wage inflexibility and the Keynesian labour supply function. *Economical Journal*, 86, 327–332.
Tversky, A., Kahneman D. (1974). Judgment under uncertainty: Heuristics and biases, *Science*, 185, 1124–1131. Reprinted in Kahneman, D. (2011). *Thinking Fast and Slow*. London: Penguin, 419–432.
Tversky, A., Kahneman, D. (1981). The framing of decisions. *Science*, 211(4481), 453–458.
Tversky, A., Kahneman, D. (1983). Extensional versus intuitive reasoning: The conjunction fallacy in probability judgement. *Psychological Review*, 90(4), 293–315.
van Praag, B., Ferrer-i-Carbonell, A. (2008). *Happiness Quantified*. Oxford: Oxford University Press.
Veblen, T. (1899). *The Theory of the Leisure Class*. New York: McMillan.
Viner, J. (1936). Nr. Keynes on the causes of unemployment. *Quarterly Journal of Economics*, 147–167. Reprinted in Lekachman (1964). *Keynes' General Theory: Reports of Three Decades*. New York: St. Martin's, 235–253.
Volcker, P. A., Harper, C. (2018). *Keeping at It. The Quest for Sound Money and Good Government*. New York: Public Affairs.

Von Neumann, J., Morgenstern, O. (1944). *Theory of Games and Economic Behavior*. Princeton: Princeton University Press.

Wansbeek, T., Kapteyn, A. (1983). Tackling hard questions by means of soft methods: The use of individual welfare functions in socioeconomic policy. *Kyklos*, 36, 249–269.

Wells, T. (2016). *Wild Man: The Life and Times of Daniel Ellsberg*. New York: Palgrave.

Wilkinson, N. (2008). *An Introduction to Behavioral Economics*. New York: Palgrave.

Winter, S. (1986). Comments on Arrow and Lucas. In: Hogarth, R., Reder, M. (eds.), *Rational Choice, The Contrast Between Economics and Psychology*. Chicago: University of Chicago Press, 243–250.

Winter-Ebner, R. (2014). What is (not) behavioral in labour economics?, *Labour Economics*, 2914, http://dx.doi.org/10.1016/j.labeco2014.07.014.

Wisman, J. (2022). Had Keynes read more Veblen: The imperative of a scientific theory of human behavior. *Preprint, American University Department of Economics Working Paper*, April.

Witt, U. (2001). Learning to consume: A theory of wants and the growth of demand. *Journal of Evolutionary Economics*, 11, 23–26.

Wren-Lewis, S. (2007). Are there dangers in the microfoundations consensus? In: Arestis, P. (ed.), *Is there a New Consensus in Macroeconomics?* Basingstoke: Palgrave, 43–60.

Young, A. (1928). Increasing returns and economic progress. *The Economic Journal*, 38(152), 527–542.

Zappa, C. (2015). Daniel Ellsberg on the Ellsberg Paradox. Manuscript, Department of Economics, University of Siena.

Zhen, Z. (2015). *A review of recent developments in research and theories of learning*. Master Thesis, University of Wuppertal.

Index

Printed and bound by CPI Group (UK) Ltd, Croydon, CR0 4YY

16/04/2025

14658434-0001